THE ONLY TRUE LIFE
Living from the Natural State

The Only True Life
Living from the Natural State

Rodney Stevens

Copyright © 2014 by Rodney Stevens

ISBN 978-1-304-36987-1

All rights reserved

Acknowledgements

In *A Short History of England*, G.K. Chesterton said that "I would maintain that thanks are the highest form of thought; and that gratitude is happiness doubled by wonder."

My immense thanks to Tim. C. Taylor for his accomplished formatting skills and ever-accommodating self-publishing assistance. I simply cannot say enough good things about him. Tim can be reached at: tctaylor@ntlworld.com. And my profound gratitude to Susan Schenck for her perceptive and fleet-footed proofreading.

That my friend, Colin Winborn, agreed to do the book's Foreword—during his summer teaching break, no less!—is a blessing all around, and I will treasure his kind words always.

My deep appreciation to John Wheeler, who patiently passed on the good news to me. And my sincere gratitude to the following individuals for their beautiful emails and generous donations: Rejane Luthemaier, Peter Kern, Railton Cabbell, Jaime Durand, Nishant Tyagi, Laith Wilson, Anoop Kumar, and John and Lesley Barlow.

Foreword ~ Graces All

In Act 3 Scene 4 of *Macbeth*, the title character—who is beginning to unravel before his appalled audience—characteristically expresses himself:

> *Then comes my fit again: I had else been perfect;*
> *Whole as the marble, founded as the rock,*
> *As broad and general as the casing air:*
> *But now I am cabined, cribbed, confined, bound in*
> *To saucy doubts and fears . . .*

In this play that—perhaps more than any other by Shakespeare—so much that seems solid and separate "vanishes into thin air" (Macbeth coined this phrase, too!). These lines perfectly capture the difference between a non-dual sensibility and that of the apparently bounded, limited self. We can feel "cabined, cribbed, confined, bound in" to the mind's monitions; or see more clearly that, at root, we are "as broad and general as the casing air"—utterly spacious, free, untouched, insubstantial. In *Measure for Measure*, Isabella speaks of how "proud man" so often misses his true nature: "Most ignorant, of what he's most assured/ His glassy essence." It is perhaps that second kind of Renaissance "glass"—the mirror—that tricks us into briefly missing our own, gloriously empty "glassiness."

I wanted to begin with these lines for two reasons: Partly because it is fascinating to see how Shakespeare intuited what have been formalised as non-dual teachings, couching them in poetic expression; but also because one of the things that Rodney and I have shared over the past year of friendship has been a love of literature. And not only literature! Our emails and Skype sessions have also charted more idiosyncratic common interests: Poetry, nature writing, vampire novels, thrillers, music, the weather, science fiction, and zombie films. And, of course, nonduality.

It has been the rarest of pleasures and privileges to make Rodney's acquaintance. Initially, I read his marvelous non-dual diary, *Fully Present,* which I heartily recommend. I was struck during our first Skype conversation by his warmth and gentle humour (always evident in his writing), as well as his unerring (and unflagging) precision when pointing to what is true. I felt an immediate kinship with him, one which has grown over a second Skype conversation, and then our subsequent email dialogue. Rodney is simply the clearest of nondual communicators, as the book you are currently holding will make abundantly evident. He has an extraordinary gift for fashioning the most resonant of pointers, which, if you let them, will pause you deeply as you read them:

"What it is that is already present?"

He also writes with utter beauty, tracing the lineaments of landscape and memory. I love the attention he pays to the natural world, to what Wordsworth called the "local habitation" of things. There is no arid abstraction. Rodney is alive to how the world of changing forms gains, if anything, a more intense colouration. And it fully felt when seen against the backdrop of the Absolute:

"Though it is December's end, the Callery pears provide a perfect motley of autumn-like hues. And like the peace and immeasurableness in which they occur, they are graces all."

What is needed, he wrote to one seeker, is an attitude of "ease and earnestness"; and this is perhaps how best to approach the writings contained herein. It is not the case that there is "nothing to do." Nor is there a need to project years of self-work to gain an "enlightened" state. The latter is already, fully, here; it just needs a little investigation to see. One might turn, momentarily, from the mirror—and see what does not need to be reflected.

Let these pointers, essays, and conversations do their work. And in no time at all, you too may recognize what is fully and wonderfully present.

Colin Winborn
Wakefield, West Yorkshire

PREFACE ~ IN NO UNCERTAIN TERMS

The American King James version of Proverbs 8-35 begins with, "For whosoever finds me finds life . . ." Barnes' *Notes on the Bible* says of this verse, "Wisdom then is the only true life." And true wisdom, of course, is knowing—in no uncertain terms—your fundamental and unvarying state.

"Who am I?" is the most important question that you could ever ask yourself. It completely transcends all aspects and nuances of science, religion, philosophy, and psychology. For the query directs you to your quintessential nature of pure awareness, to which such nondual luminaries as Ramana Maharshi, H.W.L. Poonja, Nisargadatta Maharaj, U.G. Krishnamurti, Bob Adamson, and John Wheeler have so beautifully pointed. That a reclusive, little black kid from a Lilliputian town in rural South Carolina would find his way not only to the works of the above teachers, but to the timeless Vedantic scriptures themselves is surely one of the true graces of this life.

Growing up, I found solace in books and contemplation rather than girls (they were often attractive but unreadable, and laughed—bemusedly—at my lack of interest in them), vegetables and sweets rather than meat and fish, and unbridled solitude rather than family life (not for a nano-second have I ever wanted to have children).

Clearly, a life of self-knowing was, for me (even when I was eleven and twelve years old!), the only true life, though I could not quite articulate it then. I had to find a way to earn a living, of course. But that was secondary to "enlightenment" itself, as I termed it all of those years ago. Writing came most naturally for me; hence my decision to major in English in college. Philosophy and psychology were tenacious interests too. But I simply was not a good student. I dropped out of school and began to work with my father (who was an electrician and plumber), while continuing to write essays and book reviews (for newspapers mainly), as well as to devour contemplative books, documentaries, and spiritual movies, e.g., *Fearless, Siddhartha, The Razor's Edge, Waking Life, Kumare, Wings of Desire, City of Angels, Seven Years in Tibet, Enlightenment Guaranteed, What the Bleep!?, 2001: A Space Odyssey*. That some of these films were lackluster did not seem to bother me very much.

It was enough that their context was metaphysical or transcendent, and thus delectable fodder for long, hermetic reflection in some library, bookstore, or coffee shop.

I was also drawn to Osho in those days, and I remember much of my sweat-grappled money going to purchase such richly-textured tomes such as *Heartbeat of the Absolute*; *No Water, No Moon*; *Tao: The Three Treasures*; *I Am That*; *Joshu: The Lion's Roar*; *The Book of Secrets*; and *A Cup of Tea*. I have not gone back and re-examined these works from this vantage point of presence. That would certainly be interesting to do. Alas, I no longer have any of Osho's books; I either sold them or loaned them to friends and failed to get them back. No matter. For I have moved to nonduality itself, and that is the only thing that is vital here.

Indeed, that I was actually able to recognize and to live fully (and ordinarily!) from this natural state since the spring of 2007 has been a joy beyond all expressions—though the poet in me continues to make ardent endeavors. Sometimes, however, I am content to write and utter nothing at all, and to just sit silently in this hushed and perpetual beneficence—that place from which, to quote the Advaitic scriptures, all words "fall back."

Also, it is a topic on which I cannot linger. For tears will quietly effuse. Why this body/mind reacts that way, I haven't a clue. But I am sure of one thing: That this is the only true life. It is a living reality for me, and it can be for you, as well. For there is absolutely no distant between awareness (your actual identity) and your arising notions of a separate and objective self. The "I & me" come and go. And something that comes and goes cannot possibly be your true identity. But awareness is absolute and immovable, and it is precisely what you are at this very moment. See the profound and immediate reality of that fact. Perhaps this book will help you to do just that. And if it doesn't, seek out a credible and self-realized teacher with whom you resonate. Be earnest, attentive, and gracious, and life will take it from there.

Rodney Stevens
Oct. 25, 2013
Columbia, South Carolina

Contents

Acknowledgements v
Foreword by Colin Winborn vi
Preface ix

Essays
    Assumed, But Not Actual 3
    So What Is It That You Feel? 4
    Morning Symmetry 6
    Excerpt from Fully Present 8
    Solstice 9

Discussions
    Earnestly Seeking 13
    The Right Track 15
    Why Call It Anything? 17
    Categorically Present 19
    Or So It Seems 21
    Stunningly Obvious 23
    Subtle But Obvious 25
    Instant Enlightenment 27
    How Could You Not Be Awake? 30
    To Capacity 33
    Wholly Impersonal 36
    Relaxing Your Vision 38
    Seen Clearly 40
    Utterly Unchanging 42
    A Hushed Spaciousness 45

BOOK REVIEW
Review of 'Fully Present'
by Gurleen Grewal, Ph.D 51
HAIKU 53
INTERVIEWS
Five-Question Interview 59
Assorted Questions & Answers 61
POINTERS 65

Essays

Assumed, But Not Actual

The soft, wobbly ride on the "Rapid." It lurches from the bowels of the airport to the apocalyptic grim of downtown Cleveland. I gaze through the windows. Curiosity and sadness arise within me, but not a scintilla of aversion. Dark riders loll in the dusky seats. The only whiteness holds my hand.

Later, the talk at the aromatic Coffee House at University Circle. A handful of bright writers and spiritual seekers on this frigid evening. I begin to speak. Words pour forth from a source I know all too well—and yet, not at all. For there is nothing but Presence and no one to know it. The topic tonight: "Creativity and the natural state." I could speak about this, spontaneously, for any length of time, as long as the voice holds out. It is amazing how easily any words relating to this Reality simply gush forth. It is as if there is this knowing spaciousness there that is hearing talk and perceiving the body.

Afterwards, always the second-guessing: Was I specific enough in pointing out how pauses are wellsprings for creativity? Were my examples accessible? Should I have reiterated how creativity arises in us similarly, but expresses itself differently in each person? And yet, it comes from the same source: Awareness itself.

Books are signed in my brisk, indecipherable scrawl. I glance at my name. Who is the person that toiled at these svelte tomes? One can only point to a fleeting approximation, a Beingness in which individuality appears, but is neither assumed nor is actual.

Long, tight hugs from those in attendance. Then the weighted silence with a former partner during the hurried walk to the car. She glances at me, time and again, attempting to make sense of what has "happened" to me since this understanding occurred. Her gloved hand touches my arm.

But we say nothing, as the sleet quickens. We gaze at the huge, neoclassic Cleveland Art Museum, with its white Georgian Marble and over 40,000 works of art from around globe. It is all a part of her storied life now—this sprawling, erudite, collegiate community. Her hand on my arm doesn't move. It says only one thing: Come back to me.

So What Is It That You Feel?

Breakfast on the long, sectional table from Ikea: Jumbo cinnamon muffins (from Zagara's Marketplace), Greek yogurt, melon wedges, double-pulp orange juice, Three Beans coffee for me, and piping black tea for her (the pot hidden beneath its chestnut cozy).

We periodically stare out at the fleece-like flurries of snow through the nine, multi-pane windows of her dining room. She lives here now, in this two-story, 1916 Colonial Revival house, in an up-scale Cleveland neighborhood. A trio of kitties—that remembered me within six-seconds after having not seen me for over a year—brush gracefully against my legs, marking me again and again. I reach down and stroke them, one after the other.

"So what is it that you feel?" she asked. This is the first direct question that she has ever asked about this understanding since I came to it in 2007. "Is it something like . . . contentment?"

"No," I respond, the answer instantaneous and—seemingly—coming from nowhere. "Contentment is a feeling that is easily altered. What is felt here is a presence of deep peace and spaciousness that never wavers, even with the arising of strong emotions. It is always the same because it is my natural state. It is yours, as well. It is simply a matter of your seeing it for yourself. That is all that nonduality is pointing to."

She sips her tea and gazes out the window. "I'm sorry. I should have asked you that a long time ago," she finally says.

"No apology needed," I reply. "Your interest was where it was. It may now deepen, and it may not. You can't push someone to have a vital concern with self-knowledge. Nor should you." Benign silence.

We bundle up and get into the car for sight-seeing. We drive through some of the most beautiful enclaves of city, including Shaker Heights, University Circle, Little Italy, and her own Cleveland Heights. The houses are mammoth, ranging in styles from Federal and Tudor to Georgian and grandiose Queen Anne. They were mostly built in the early 20th-century, when the rich preferred their living spaces cavernous.

We then make mouth-watering forays to Trader Joe's, Heinen's, and On the Rise Artisan Breads, where we get a loaf of oven-fresh Country

Sourdough for "Cousin Amy," where we are going for dinner that afternoon.

Amy and her family of doctors: Her husband is a psychiatrist, and their two sons are, respectively, an internist and orthopedic surgeon. And each has children who love to descend upon this rambling, two-story lake house, that sits within twenty-feet of a dizzying cliff. Sleet quickens as we pull into the drive. The amber-lit windows are adorned with warmth, movement, and people wanting to meet and talk with me.

But as I get out the car, I am thoroughly paused by the stormy and seemingly endless slate expanse of Lake Erie. "Make my apologies," I say and run to the long, deeply angled steps leading down to the beach. "Rodney!" she yells. But I am gone, holding tightly on to wobbly wooden railings. I slip three times on the icy steps, but manage to right myself and continue the slow, perilous descent.

The beach is tiny and cluttered. Wave-flattened stones, tree limbs, boat detritus, seaweeds, and coyote tracks predominate. Four black, partially-submerged, metal groins stave off the house's eventual tumble into the bone-chilling waters. The air reeks of oil, rot, and fish. And far out, the grey, gelid churning of the lake melds with a turbulent sky. I turn and gaze upward to the house. And there they are—women at the window, staring down, protectively.

"So what is it that you feel?" she asked. Utter vastness . . .and gratitude.

Morning Symmetry

I sit on the blue bench by the blue table on the red deck. It's not even dawn. Freshly-grounded Kona coffee with caramel macchiato creamer steams in my mug. I am in the back of her small, new house. The yard has its own perfect symmetry: The casual and up-turned water buckets directly across from me; the pumpkin-colored broom angled against the redwood railing; the slew of gray shavings from lime-tinted Sycamore limbs; and the canary Malibu chair, across which a purple twist mop has dried into its own speckless calm.

And how could I forget the redolent pots of Rosemary, Catnip, and Greek Oregano (into which she instructed me to pour the old water from the cat's bowl)? The temperature will reach 105 F today. But there is no hint of the morning coolness.

On the table sits a small, brown Buddha that she purchased for me. It is neither expensive nor unique, thank goodness—just an ordinary but beautiful half-foot figurine from a local Tuesday Morning shop. I saw a picture of it somewhere and smiled. That she remembered my smile is astonishing to me. The Buddha is compact and gilded, with numinous, half-closed eyes. Seekers sit this way in hopes of reaching their own transcendence, not realizing that it is the other way around: You first see or understand that you are Transcendence. Then the eyes are naturally calm. Indeed, mine are now at their most relaxed when half-closed.

I could sit interminably like this, on the blue bench by the brown Buddha. Stillness within stillness. But then, minutes later, a Cardinal darts and trills; and I watch a huge cellar spider make its way to the dew-dampened roof to temper its web. The stillness returns. For how long I have no idea.

Then she is there, tall and pale inside the half-opened back door. She smiles, as her eyes focus from the depths of dreams. Her Charleston green t-shirt—covering just to the top of her thighs—is too heavy for summer. She sweats in her sleep but is deeply content. With perfect, middle-aged symmetry, she touches the bottom of the door with her sleep-waxened foot, making sure that it is ajar for the cats. But somehow, the door simply stays that way. As do you, my dear reader. There isn't even a door. Just Openness. Always and only—bare and utter Openness. And you are That.

Excerpt from 'Fully Present: Daily Reflections on Nonduality':

Wednesday, May 19

I am enjoying Ian McEwan's *Solar*, about a brilliant, Nobel Prize-winning physicist whose best work is behind him, and whose fifth marriage is in terrible shape because of his compulsive womanizing. Here is a particularly beautiful quote from a fellow scientist who is attempting to get Beard (the physicist) to consider taking a hard look at solar energy:

"The [sun] drenches our planet, drives our climate and its life. A sweet rain of photons, and all we have to do is hold out our cups!"

How lovely, that. And all we have to do is simply recognize the actually of awareness. For it is our everything. And no real effort is required—just a simple seeing of what has always been bountifully present!

Solstice

And now, the gradual lengthening of days, rather than the primal darkness of an approaching winter. It is effortless—the planet's tilting—but is registered here through some elemental knowingness. Oh, how I have treasured the snug twilights and the bright, ephemeral days.

Gone (or nearly so) are the scarlet ovals of the Callery Pears and the lemon-light on the Florida Maples, both of which I would get out of the security truck to touch, as if to imbibe their hues. Someone would stop and ask directions to the movie theater, and I would point to this immediate resplendence. "Oh yeah," the driver would dryly offer. I would smile at his unknowing eyes and give precise directions to the cinema.

In Barnes and Noble, I get water in the cafe. At one of the tables sits an attractive and diminutive American Buddhist nun, working at her laptop. As I am leaving, she glances up at me, frowns acutely, and then re-focuses on her ancient Dell. Is it my security uniform? Or does she know me from my books and blog, and sees me as the anti-Buddha?

But I am not anti-anything! And "There is no multiplicity here," as the scriptures rightly posit, despite any appearances to the contrary, whether they be man and woman, or Buddhist nun and very ordinary guy. All is Presence.

Outside, gunmetal clouds extend from horizon-to-horizon. Flicker of remembrance. Another solstice: I loved our balcony in Montreal, just off Boulevard St.-Laurent. The entire alley, three-stories below, lay plumed with snow. On our first morning, as you showered, I stepped out onto the ebony grate that was adorned with alabaster wedges from the midnight storm. Gingerly, I cupped my coffee to warm my hands and thought of you inside—the water caressing every part of you, just as I had done throughout the Siberian night.

We had eaten at Schwartz's Deli, to nourish your "starved Jewish roots," you joked. You had some kind of medium-smoked meat on rye and I an egg salad sandwich, of which I only ate half—for I could not stop gazing at you . . .Our break-up was as benumbing as the air that I was feeling on that arctic balcony—the arguments, the separation, and then the heart-wrenching, single-line email: "You should know that I am now seeing someone else."

I pause to search for that decade year-old pain . . .and not a scintilla can be found—only the full memory itself. No flutters of heartache or angst. That kind of attachment is gone for me now. Multiplicity has ceased, though still appreciated—even reveled in! It is a kind of Love after love. But this one is unceasing, impersonal, and wholly without measure. And it never disappoints. Right here and now, peer into your very own wonder. Absolutely no one can give you that.

Dialogues

EARNESTLY SEEKING

Questioner: Hey, Rodney. I just saw on CNN that the Republican candidates are heading your way for the South Carolina primaries. So I thought I would drop you a line and see how you're holding up.

Rodney: Primaries? What primaries? It's news to me. I'm joking, of course. But as you might guess, I don't follow politics. I am not advocating that sentiment for anyone. It is just me. I'm no example for anybody.

Q: I also wanting to let you know how much I'm really enjoying 'A Vastness All Around' and 'Fully Present'. Both have been very helpful on several issues.

Rodney: I'm happy to hear that. Thank you—and thank you for the purchases, as well!

Q: In your diary, for example, you cleared away the doubts and fears that came up when reading—many years ago—'Krishnamurti's Notebook'. You show that this understanding can be something natural, and that the family does not have to suffer from dramatic changes.

Rodney: And neither did J. Krishnamurti, I imagine. Still, I found his writing vague and dualistic. But he appears to have been a lovely and immensely compassionate person. And I, like many former seekers, have several of his books.

Q: I'm in my late 50's, and deeply saddened over the fact that after years of earnest looking and direct pointing from credible teachers, there is no final understanding here. And I know that it may happen soon, or it may not.

Rodney: Yes, but just to be clear: Awareness has happened! Awareness is all there is. In fact, it is so in evidence that you are overlooking it. And I am not pointing you out here. This "by-passing" of presence is going on in all spiritual sectors, with seekers the world over. That timeless and marvelously concise nondual gem You Are That points us to an immediacy to which you have never given your attention. And when you do come to your clear seeing, you will certainly perceive that there never was a who, but always a what—awareness itself.

Q: Yes, I see what you're saying. And I'm certainly not asking you what can be done because that would be a practice or a path, which would be a separate "me" operating at some level.

Rodney: Right—there can be no path or process to what you already are.

Q: I'm not even interested in a career and material things. I just want to know the truth of who I am.

Rodney: Food, clothing, and shelter are paramount. Once you have the essentials, then it's a personal decision as to the quality and quantity of those things. Your forging ahead is commendable. Just keep in mind that there is no "ahead" and no place to go. Presence is ever-present. And you never move from being what you are right at this moment. Any pause or pointer can "take" you there—that is, point you to something that is supremely present. And time is not a factor in that recognition. So what is it, right now, that isn't changing and that you need no time to see?

THE RIGHT TRACK

Question: In a recent blog entry, you say to "Simply bring your attention to the spaciousness in which the I-sense comes and goes, and you will be on the right track."

Rodney: That's correct.

Q: Could you say a bit more about what you mean by "attention"? I'd always thought of attention as being a mental function of the character or person. Presumably you're using the word attention in a different sense.

Rodney: Again, you presume correctly. :)

Q: Right, because the spaciousness that you are speaking of isn't a thing or object that "I" can place my attention on in the same way that I give my attention on a piece of music or a book, for example. So presence-awareness is undeniably present, but how can I put my attention on it?

Rodney: Very nicely put. If you remain with this line of insights, you won't need me at all!

Q: Well, the insights stop right there, unfortunately. And I'm just left with that all-consuming question—how do I place my attention on awareness?

Rodney: By recognizing that it is present. It seems easier to give your attention to a piece of beautiful music or writing than to awareness itself because—in those examples—you are naturally and habitually utilizing your hearing and seeing. You don't even think about it. But awareness is not an object; so you have to bring your attention to it in a completely different manner. One of the ways of doing that is with the following question: What is it that is fully present, but that you need no senses to see?

Q: Ah, yes . . . I can feel the stillness within that question.

Rodney: And that peripheral stillness is pointing to your ultimate stillness. They are actually one and the same. Just take a close and easy look at the pause itself, keeping in mind that this is not a mental action at all. No thought or action will help you at this point. It is staying with the pause that's paramount. And if done correctly, you will discern that this moment of quietude is actually the presence of awareness to which all the great sages and teachers have spoken. There is really no "shifting" of any sort; but rather, a simple and easy discovery—indeed, a kind of coming home.

Q: Thank you, Rodney. I want nothing more than that.

WHY CALL IT ANYTHING?

Question: Hi, Rodney. I have been reading and enjoying your books, as well as John Wheeler's 'Awakening to the Natural State'. What I find so surprising and refreshing is the way you both keep returning to the simplicity of observing what's really happening, not giving in to the mind's attempts to "figure it out." Instead, just attend to presence.

Rodney: Right. The mind is in no position to either comprehend awareness or to witness it. Indeed, it arises wholly within awareness.

Q: The simplicity of your directions seems to be working. I am going to attempt to describe what is being seen here, and I wonder if you could please comment.

Rodney: Sure.

Q: First, it is so simple that it is nearly impossible to describe. Mostly, there is a strong sense of presence, which is clearly awareness. It is silent, with nothing at all to say. It is entirely at peace with itself.

Rodney: Very good—and that is nicely articulated, by the way.

Q: There is no movement, no desire to move, no sense of anything desired or required for completeness. It is also quite obvious that this present awareness, this "no thing," is at the center of everything, is what I might want to call "me" except for the hilarious fact that "I" don't really exist.

Rodney: Again, all on-the-mark.

Q: Of course I must at the same time say that "I am." But it really seems that the "I" is utterly unimportant.

Rodney: It is, to a substantial degree. But our temporary sense-of-self allows us to function in life. Whether it's writing, speaking, paying our bills, or arranging a lunch get-together, our provisional "self" functions as the apparent doer. But the doer is just a thought, and a thought is not a conscious entity. It only appears to be sentient because presence is shining through it.

Q: Exactly. And it seems better to just call it presence or present awareness and be done with it. Or even better, why call it anything? It just IS. It always is, and it is always the same utterly quiet, peaceful sense of being. Why the need to name it?

Rodney: We name it in order to speak about it or to point to it. We also name it because we want others to understand what we are talking about when we talking about awareness proper. For we are not conversing about the dogwood tree in the front yard or even everyday consciousness, of course. We are pointing to something that is ceaseless, and that is our natural and luminous state.

Q: I do find that mind comes in and distracts attention from presence now and then.

Rodney: That's going to happen. Your body is going to continue to react to stimuli from your surroundings, and thoughts are going to appear as a result of those reactions. Presence does not disappear; rather, your attention momentarily goes to other things. But you never move from being awareness itself. And awareness never moves from being absolutely present. So the question becomes: What is it, right now, that is always the same? When the answer to that question is recognized, you most certainly will never lose it.

Categorically Present

Question: "You are seeking something that is always present" is a powerful pointer, and this is what I've been asking myself over the past few days. In the waking state, experiencing is happening all the time. And for experiencing to occur, awareness must be present.

Rodney: Correct.

Q: So all of this seems very natural—experiencing is happening, thoughts arise, and sensations come and go, as do perceptions. What's really amusing is to watch the coming up of the thought, "I'm getting closer to understanding this," because awareness is no closer or any more distant than it has ever been!

Rodney: Precisely. Self-inquiry is not progressive. You can't make any step-by-step approaches to Reality, despite what 99% of the world's spiritual teachers say. Awareness never varies from being categorically present. Your ego or sense-of-self cannot "move" toward awareness because they are temporary appearances in it. Upon recognizing or understanding that, you immediately begin to see that your life is being lived from this state of unchanging Beingness. Feelings and emotions continue to arise, but they no longer define you.

Q: It is really starting to dawn on me now how awareness is obviously present, but it's not something that can be grasped as an object. That has been a source of frustration for me in the past.

Rodney: You were trying to lasso it, instead of saying, "Wait a minute. Enough is enough. This isn't working." So the question then becomes, "What is it—right here and now—that I do not have to attain"? The answer to that question has to be something that never alters in any manner. So your body, mind, thoughts, personality, senses, and consciousness are automatically out of the picture. They can't possibly be who and what you are because all of those things change. But what doesn't? What is it, at this very moment, that Is Not Moving? It is awareness. And it never varies from being unambiguously present. So it has to be your essence! Thus, your body, mind, thoughts, personality, senses, and consciousness are automatically out of the picture. They cannot possibly be you are because all of those things change. But what doesn't? What is it, as you are reading these words, that Is . . .Not . . .Moving?

Q: So instead of trying to grasp it, I've been simply living with those potent pointers of yours, precisely like the question above—"What is it—right here and now—that I don't have to attain"?

Rodney: Excellent. Mull it over, allow it to naturally halt your thinking and conceptualizing. And within that pause is a presence of awareness that—because of its obviousness—you have neglected to recognized. I am not pointing you out particularly. I'm merely addressing the fact that there is nothing to grasp, and that awareness has never not been present. See the truth and obviousness of this, and there won't be anything to ponder or contemplate. Presence will simply be there, as it always has been.

OR SO IT SEEMS

Question: Hi Rodney. I'm really enjoying 'Fully Present: Daily Reflections on Nonduality'. It's like I'm right there with you, from day to day.

Rodney: You poor woman.

Q: Oh, no! The way you weave nonduality into your daily entries is really beautiful. I was able to get these great new insights into awareness from your everyday settings. And your detailed food descriptions kept making me hungry!

Rodney: Thanks! I'm happy to hear that you are enjoying it.

Q: There has been no "final understanding" yet. But that's okay. I'm prepared for the long haul. Didn't you read one of John Wheeler's books a dozen times before you got it?

Rodney: Yes, but that's just the way it happened. Everyone comes to this seeing differently. It may occur on your very next re-read. Or it may come while you are working at your desk, blowing your nose, gardening, or having a cup of tea or coffee. There is really no predicting it. Further, time is not a factor in this. It just isn't. So preparing for "the long haul" is a projection that you can forget about. Also, any talk of time is a way for the ego—that temporary sense of individuality—to sneak and borrow into the mix of things. And neither it nor years of any kind of practice can help you to witness your abiding clarity.

Q: Okay. I already know that efforts and practices are not the way to approach this.

Rodney: Precisely. Because awakening—or whatever term you prefer to use—is merely a matter of seeing something that has always been one-hundred percent present. Any methodology or goal-oriented action toward it is, in reality, a move away from it. So when you are told this by a reputable source, you are paused by the enormity of three things: That the source has perceived this fundamental clarity in him or herself, that awareness is immediately present, and that no progressive steps are necessary to recognize it. So go with the pause. What is it revealing to you? What is present when no thought is present?

Q: Well, nothing. Or so it seems. Then another thought rises, and I curse myself for missing awareness.

Rodney: That "so it seems" is apropos. For awareness is abundantly there. However, when it's bypassed, another thought comes up, the one in which you are "cursing" yourself. But if you get swept up with such castigation, you are going with the thought or the feeling rather than with that momentary respite between them. Also, awareness never disappears, even when your attention is on a thought or an emotion. So there is nothing to wait for and nothing to get. And there is certainly nothing to curse yourself about. For you are what you are at this very moment. Awakening is comparable to suddenly seeing the Mona Lisa in one of those 3D pictures of squiggly lines and circles. You were told that the face was always present. But now you are seeing it for yourself. And nothing could be more beautiful.

Q: Oh, Rodney, I can't tell you how I look forward to seeing that smile.

Rodney: The smile is happening right now. And you are it! See the immediate reality of this, or reflect upon anything that we have talked about here, when you feel an inclination to do so. And remember, we are speaking about something that is clear, immediate, and effortless. You do not have to "reach" or "attain" one single thing. Nothing! Everything that you need is directly within you. Indeed, you are it.

STUNNINGLY OBVIOUS

Question: Hi Rodney. I'm continuing to enjoy and resonate with your powerful pointers.

Rodney: Thank you.

Q: In your recent blog entry, I was particularly moved by your, "Even to say 'Just be' is a directive towards some fruitless action."

Rodney: Yes, it subtly implies that there is someone who can move closer to some imagined state. But Beingness is what we are. Therefore, it cannot be grasped or acquired.

Q: And it can never be lost either, I gather.

Rodney: Exactly. Nothing is missing except your recognition of something that is categorically present all the time. And this fact tends to cause a double reaction in seekers: First, there is this sudden relaxation, because you are being told (by a credible source) that meditating, mantras, mindfulness, and New-Age maxims to "Just be" aren't going to help you with self-knowing—that all of your exhaustive practices and approaches are for naught. Indeed, they will simply cloud the issue. And second, there is an unanticipated curiosity about what it is, precisely, that has always been in place.

Q: For some years, back in the 70s and early 80s, I was involved with a group that laid extraordinary significance on the experience gained in meditation, but never questioned who was having the experience. You go and sit on your special cushion, in your special room where your special incense is burning and your special piece of music is playing: it's all "mind stuff!" It's all experiencing.

Rodney: It's all experiences and "mind stuff." And no thought, action, or intellectual activity has any relationship to awareness, which is totally beyond all physical and mental activities. And yet, presence is nothing more than your ordinary, everyday awareness, which is what you are right now. That is one of the keys to the non-puzzle: That presence is the whatness or the knowingness that is existing within and as you at this very moment. But people take themselves to be their bodies, minds, consciousness, and even their personalities. So when most of these individuals become interested in spirituality, they automatically attempt to use their thinking or physicality to "acquire" something that they supposedly do not currently possess. And self-realization just does not happen that way.

Q: That's one of the reasons I like your blog. You hone in on the non-relationship between practices and awareness.

Rodney: And the same applies to experiences, of course. Grander experiences do not equate to a deeper or more solid understanding of your essential nature. Indeed, there is no understanding at all in such cases. It's just the experiencing of experiences!

Q: Again and again.

Rodney: As for the 70s and 80s, I think I was doing some of the same things that you were in this fervent attempt to "acquire" enlightenment. But absolutely nothing came of it. For what we were seeking is fully and magnificently present. It always has been, and it always will be. But because we thought of self-knowing in terms of "enlightenment" (i.e., that it is something for which we have to strive, and it is going to take a certain amount of time to "get" it), we bypass the stunningly obvious.

Q: Thank you, Rodney. I hope this finds you well. And I'll be in touch at a later date, if that's okay?

Rodney: No problem. Take care.

Subtle But Obvious

Question: Rodney, I just finished reading John Wheeler's words in 'The Light Behind Consciousness', where he says, "All you can say about yourself is 'I am' and 'I know' and 'I am nothing perceivable or conceivable'." I'm not exactly sure why, but those sentences were very calming to me.

Rodney: Well, there could be any number of reasons for that, aside from the words' clarity and truthfulness. The things that are perceivable are constantly changing. But the "I am-ness" that is recognizing those changes is not altering in the least. So anything that is perceivable can't possibly be you. So yes, "I am" or "I know" is pretty much all that you can realistically utter about yourself, with the former being particularly on the mark. Everything else is just an add-on, e.g., "I am man/woman," "I am a banker," "I am my body," "I am a wretched soul," "I am an American/Canadian—"

Q: I am unenlightened.

Rodney: I am unenlightened. I am my ego, and on and on. But something is knowing that those thoughts and assumptions are temporarily there. What is that something? That is the question that should be centered upon, if you truly want to discover the answer to what you are. It is a magnificent question because it naturally pauses you. You feel the beauty of its significance, even if the answer to the question remains unclear. The pause is pointing you to your essence, to your own innate clarity and spaciousness. And given that it is innate, it is nothing that you can "practice" your way to. You are what you are, as we are speaking, right here and now. And you never move from that, despite all notions otherwise.

Q: Right. I read John's statements about two hours ago, and the tranquilness is still there. Also, the truth of the words has become clearer. It was subtle at first, but then, by itself, a stillness grew and it became far more obvious. Still subtle, but obvious.

Rodney: Sounds nice.

Q: *Well, that's what I'm getting at, I suppose. I'm sitting here before the computer and all is peace and gentleness, like the quiet gladness of a young child at home, surrounded by an unseen love that is fully known and cherished without words. Is this just another in a long, long line of experiences? Or is this Presence? Anything is possible, I suppose.*

Rodney: Indeed it is. But I'm fairly certain that what is occurring is an experience, though a deeply calming and reflective one. And such occasions, while temporary, can point you to an even deeper stillness, that is right there for the seeing. And this, of course, is a stillness from which you never move. That "peace" is what you are, and that you are articulating and feeling some semblance of it can easily lead you towards a final seeing and understanding of the matter. No sustained or concentrated efforts are needed for this. You neither have to close your eyes nor move into any kind of special position. For awareness is perfectly present before any of those things are done! So why bother? Why waste a millisecond (or a lifetime!) indulging in any action that is on the mental or physical level? Awareness is neither waiting nor hiding. And there is absolutely nothing to cultivate or to "bring out." All of that stuff is simply false, spiritual lore. And no matter how tantalizing the stories and anecdotes, they are just experiences, every single one of them.

Q: *Well, now that I've been properly thrashed—*

Rodney: Oh, no! That wasn't my intent at all!

Q: *Just kidding. Thanks, Rodney. I'd love to set up another phone consultation, if I may? Hearing your voice seems to help me to get a better handle on all of this.*

Rodney: Sure thing. Looking forward to it.

Instant Enlightenment

Question: Greetings, Rodney. I am new to nonduality, but I really love your blog. Your writing is so beautiful and direct.

Rodney: Thank you!

Q: And just so I understand you correctly, you're the guy that offers instant enlightenment, right?

Rodney: Oh, absolutely! (Laughing.) But then, "enlightenment" is always instantaneous. It doesn't piecemeal itself out to you. And why would it? Awareness is without any division whatsoever; and you are awareness itself. Right at this moment, you are That. You are not this defined person who suddenly (or progressively) "becomes" your natural identity. So enlightenment is nothing that I can give or offer because it is your fundamental nature. And you can't get what you already are! Ponder that statement when you are so inclined. It is one of the golden keys to Self-knowledge.

Q: Okay. Thanks for clearing that up.

Rodney: Also, "enlightenment" doesn't work as a word or description when it comes to this understanding. It gives the impression that you are attaining something special and other-worldly, when what we are speaking about is your core existence. Nonduality directs you to the stuff of this world, to your own, everyday life, which you take to be flat, dimensionless, and ordinary. But it has an extraordinary essence and background to it, and that is your natural and ever-present state.

Q: So I need to "not meditate" more on that background! (Laughing).

Rodney: All that is needed is the recognition of it, of that unchanging presence of peace and spacious that is thoroughly before and within you. Again, we are speaking about your natural state here, and not the thoughts, emotions, and sensations that arise in that state. And that is what nonduality is about all: It is a timeless teaching that directs you to your fundamental nature. I am merely someone who was fortunate enough to see where Shankara, Lao Tzu, Ramana Maharshi, Nisargadatta, Bob Adamson, and John Wheeler were pointing. And what a splendid state it is.

Q: I'm really thrilled for you, Rodney. And I want that for myself, as well.

Rodney: Well, nothing could be simpler. I know I keep saying that, but it is the bare, utter truth. For we are talking about something that is both fully present and is what you are as you are reading these words. Given that, any kind of action, meditation, or technique to move you "towards" self-knowledge is not going to work. Why? Because you then will just be moving away from it, so to speak. For the idea of "enlightenment" is very much like a mirage in the desert: Water appears to be directly ahead. But nothing is actually there, except your concept or notion about it, along with, perhaps, an experience or two.

Q: And that concept or experience isn't going to help me much.

Rodney: When you are focused upon a concept or any idea about anything, it's still in the mind. You are merely thinking about awareness rather than noticing or understanding its immediate presence. For awareness is closer than our own skin, and yet we miss it. We give heed and homage to glorious houses, important-sounding titles, problematic relationships, and shallow spiritual retreats rather than to genuine Self-knowing.

Q: Amen on those problematic relationships!

Rodney: Life, for 99.99 percent of people, is going from one experience to another. Some experiences are pleasurable, and others are not. And then there is everything in between. But there is far more to living than this! There is the matter, for one thing, of seeing that your life is being lived—and not by this self-important "you" but by Existence itself. You're a wave on the ocean of limitlessness. Why not see that fully for yourself and have a direct sense of who and what you are? You are the ocean, you are the infinitude. Those aren't concepts or fanciful thoughts. They are clear and glorious facts.

How Can You Not Be Awake?

Question: Oh, Rodney. What a sad and funny joke this searching business is!

Rodney: It needn't be. But yes, in most cases, it certainly is.

Q: It's like a phantom searching for a phantom.

Rodney: Right. And yet, nothing could be less a phantom than our everyday awareness.

Q: Thanks for the reassurance! In theory, I see what you are saying. As I am this completely free and non-conceptual awareness itself, how can there possibly be an "I" to participate in a search?

Rodney: Precisely. And the "I" or sense-of-self, is the phantom. Again, there is only a sense-of-self there, not an actual one. And that fact alone has a very powerful resonance.

Q: Right.

Rodney: So on one hand, there can be this careful reasoning which can lead to direct understanding or recognition of your natural state. And other the on hand, your thoughts or notions about awareness really don't matter. They may be incorrect or they may be dead-on. But fundamentally, they are of little consequence because—

Q: They are just thoughts and ideas. Right.

Rodney: And all beliefs and debates surrounding self-knowledge (whether the perspectives are Buddhist, Zen Buddhist, Taoist, Christian, or nondual) are operating on a conceptual level. And yet, all of the previous frames of spiritual references have their nuggets of truth. But they are not the truths themselves. They are merely pointing to your very own radiance.

Q: I like how you raise the point in your writings about how can you not be awake!

Rodney: Which promptly pauses you.

Q: And before the next question appears, I am already here, this presence of awareness. I have read it a hundred times and not grasped the reality of it. So I would greatly appreciate an opportunity to have a phone consultation with you.

Rodney: Certainly. We then would be able to quickly pinpoint whatever issues that need clarifying, as well as address any impromptu questions you might have.

Q: And whatever I'm doing wrong, feel free to tell me to stop it!

Rodney: Well, it is more about overlooking the obvious, rather than being right or wrong. Awareness is what you are. But you are scanning the horizons, being captivated by this and that. (And maybe not you, personally. I am speaking about the general way of things with today's seekers.) But however beautiful and tantalizing the sights, thoughts, and sensations may be, they pale in comparison to your own innate peace and brilliance. It is boundless and unchanging. And you are precisely That right at this moment. So it is not a matter of your someday "becoming" it or having some grand, future, visionary event. There is nothing to procure—or even to hope for! But just to be clear, it is perfectly fine to want this understanding. Just be mindful of the point that you are wanting something that you one-hundred percent already are.

Q: I really like that. It's beautiful, and it momentarily stops my thinking cold.

Rodney: Remain with the pause and beauty. What is it that you are seeing? See how it directly points you to your true identity—at this moment. Forget about tomorrow. Tomorrow is a thought; it's the mind and "me" in full operation. What is it, right now, that is utterly hushed, unvarying, and clarity itself?

To Capacity

Q: Hi, Rodney. This is my first email ever to a spiritual teacher and author!

Rodney: Thank you!

Q: I am really struck by the directness and simplicity and persistence of your pointers.

Rodney: I'm delighted that they resonate with you.

Q: I'm in my sixties and live in [names European country]. When I was nineteen, I had an amazing series of experiences. I'll be happy to share them with you, if you like.

Rodney: Sure, if you'd like to.

Q: I awoke one morning with the most wondrous feelings of peace and well-being. Scintillating feelings of joy became my moment to moment experience. There was also deep clarity and fullness. It pervaded every cell in my being. For the first time ever, I felt totally free and alive! I saw myself now as part of the flow of the universe. Deep feelings of love and compassion for all of life filled me to capacity.

Rodney: It sounds beautiful.

Q: Thoughts seemed to be mechanical and stale—the immediacy of the Now was where life was! There was also the realisation that everyone and everything was connected. And everything had meaning. Prior to this, I hated getting up in the morning. But now, after only a few hours of restful sleep, my energy levels soared, and I couldn't wait to see what the day would bring! Also, wave after wave of insights continued to arise, and I seemed to live in what can only be described an enormous sea of love.

Rodney: Again, very nice.

nind came back in and began dismantling the joy, ıs scattered into thousands of different pieces . . . I perience when you were twelve or fourteen, that All Around', which I greatly enjoyed. Can you tell ve were experiencing? It would also be nice get it

Rodney: What we both experienced were simply experiences. Yes, they were powerful, intuitive, penetrating, and even awe-inspiring. But they were experiences nonetheless. I am not attempting to totally discount them, but rather, to give them an accurate assessment. Some people call them "awakening experiences" and other label them as "awakenings." I only reserved the term "awakening" for a sudden and unwavering recognition of your natural state. It is a recognition that doesn't change in the least. It's unfortunate that many people who have such occurrences promptly pronounce themselves as fully awake or having had that final understanding. Nothing could be further from the truth. But that's their bandwagon, and I wish them nothing but Happy Trails.

Q: *I like that.*

Rodney: Such experiences, though, can be instrumental in spurring one on to true self-knowledge. I know that that was certainly the case with me. But no experience, however psychic or visionary, was captivating enough to pull me away from this quest for a fundamental understanding of both myself and of life. And I was certainly guilty—all of those years ago—of labeling the intention of my quest as Enlightenment. But in the spring of 2007, I clearly saw that there is no separate individual to be enlightened at all! All there was was my natural state, which was one of enduring peace and spaciousness. And that natural state was and is pristine awareness, from which one never moves. Thus, you are already what you are seeking. So any notions of practices, methods, or spiritual journeys can be promptly thrown out the window.

Q: *I see that so clearly now—how any practice is just a heap of rubbish.*

Rodney: And you mentioned wanting to get those transcendental experiences back—

Q: *Well, not so much anymore—and that insight occurred in these very few minutes!*

Rodney: Excellent. Because any experience—by its very nature—is transitory. However glorious it may be, it isn't going to be able to help you with knowing who and what you are. For experiences, among other things, have no inherent intelligence. They are insentient, lifeless. But what is that presence of awareness that is witnessing all of these appearances? What is that presence of awareness that is staring you in the face at this very moment? It is right here, right now. Come back to that point and question, throughout your day and afternoon, if you are drawn to do so. Because the answer is you—your very own nature.

WHOLLY IMPERSONAL

Question: Hi, Rodney. Just a quick message to say that I hope the operation to remove your wisdom tooth went ok! I had to have a couple removed two of years ago. I remember my cheeks swelling up so much afterwards that I resembled a hamster! :)

Rodney: Great to hear from you! Hope things in the U.K. are going well. It turns out that no dental surgery was necessary. They were able to do a straight exaction. And there was no swelling! I'm still taking Ibuprofen a couple of times a day and using the prescription dental rinse. But I seem to be recovering okay, knock on wood.

Q: Terrific . . . And thank you, as ever, for the latest pointers on your blog. They are so clear and clean and beautiful, especially "What is it that does not know your name?" That paused me powerfully. There was just this luminous, aware, empty presence that was registering the question.

Rodney: Just remain with that empty, aware, luminousity. Or rather, see that you actually never move from it—that it is always there, whether your attention goes to your coffee cup or to the clarity.

Q: Yes, that's it. It doesn't appear to remain. But when it's there, it is at once wholly impersonal and wholly intimate. I can sense it as these words flow across the screen. It is not localised to a body, not separate from anything, but equally, not affected by anything. I'll just keep coming back to this, and noticing it until the realisation is clear.

Rodney: That's certainly one way of going about it. Whatever you feel drawn to do, do. Just stay mindful of the fact that awareness doesn't move or change in least. And that it is merely being overlooked, that's all. We have all been taught that we are this and that. The list is endless: Man, woman, Englishman, Christian, Buddhist, Alaskan, my personality, consciousness, reincarnating soul, etc.

The Only True Life

Q: Nondualist!

Rodney: Particularly nondualist!. . .But fundamentally, you are none of those things. You are pure awareness. This is your abiding reality, this is what never varies. Everything else is just transitional appearances, whether it be your body, your personality, or your consciousness. Further, if you were just any of those things, you wouldn't have the ability to know it. For none of those things have inherent intelligence. Thus, no self-reflection would be possible if you were merely your physicality or some state of consciousness.

Q: I find that whenever the mind is looked to as any kind of authority, there is apparent suffering. This is also the case when I get caught up in questions about karma, reincarnation, different paths and practices etc. Whenever any of this is given any weight, presence (seemingly) fades, or is obscured. The mind is hungry for confusion, for clutter; it will feed on anything.

Rodney: Good points, all. So you are clearly seeing how the mind and practices can't possibly bring you lasting peace. The mind and certain yoga practices, for instance, certainly have their place. And I don't want to sound as if I am totally discounting them, because I am not. I am merely saying that true peace and clarity comes with the recognition of your immediate presence of awareness. Thoughts and emotions arise in that awareness and disappear. Thus, they are fleeting and dualistic nature. But your true innateness is not. You are the eternal witness, so to speak—that supreme intelligence to which Lao Tzu, Jesus, and Nisaradatta Maharai so beautifully pointed.

Q: Thanks, Rodney. And I thoroughly enjoyed our talk!

Rodney: As did I! Take care.

Relaxing Your Vision

Question: Hi, Rodney. I have just been re-reading sections of 'A Vastness All Around', and I'm finding each reading is totally fresh and vibrant.

Rodney: Happy to hear it. Additional readings of nondual books, blogs, and Web sites can be immensely helpful in getting a handle on nonduality—especially if those works are pointing beyond the page and the computer screen. For one of the many glories of this teaching is that it is directing you to what you are at this very moment, and not to some mystical experience or "attainable" state. You are awareness. So there is nothing to get or to reach. So as you continue to read, keep in mind that the answer is within you and not within the words. What you are looking for is a hushed and undeniable presence of peace and spaciousness.

Q: I keep finding new gems in the book! This sentence in "Slow the Boat" really stopped me this time:

> *"Relaxing your vision, you see that because of the light's refraction through the water, the bay is not at all shallow, but remarkably deep."*

This is such a beautiful and resonant metaphor. It reminded me that this understanding has nothing to do with effort, straining or mental contortion—all of which come inevitably with the mind's involvement.

Rodney: Precisely. It's the mind in operation. And the mind is not going to get it. When you are told (by a realized source) that consciousness can't possibly be who and what you are because consciousness changes, the mind is naturally paused. It just happens, because all along there has been this assumption that you were one of those things. And when you are further told that your true nature has to be something that never varies in the least, you are paused again, because the mind has no conceptual handle for that. So reflecting upon the above truths and pointers, the mind stops. Then awareness—in the form of serenity and expansiveness—can be easily recognized. And one of the very first things that you understand is that it has always been fully present.

Q: Exactly. In the past, I tried very hard to "see" or "get" this, which has left me frustrated. But the moment I "relax my vision"—lovely phrase!—it is so radiantly, naturally clear. It is already here, and just needs re-acquaintance. And it doesn't even need this!

Rodney: No, it doesn't. Just see that those moments of clarity are always present. You don't need to get re-acquainted at all. It may seem that way now. But with a little clear seeing, you will be able to recognize that this state of yours is—as the words indicate—naturally and unequivocally present.

Q: When my "vision" is "relaxed", there is that subtle, undeniable sense of knowing—in which thoughts, sensations and perceptions arise. These are all known—by what? I find myself naturally asking, "What is it that knows these thoughts?", and pausing with that question, noticing the changeless space.

Rodney: Let go of the question and bring your attention to the pause. As long as you are centered on the question, you are immersed in thought. You are remaining on a conceptual level. But you are the pause, you see. You are the Pause. That "changeless space" is you. And that changeless space is no void. It only appears so at first glance. But its depth is immeasurable, and it is replete with peace and plenitude. Just a slight "relaxation" is all that is needed. And then all will be made clear.

Q: Thank you again, Rodney! And take good care. Your writing, and that of John Wheeler's, are really helping clarify this so much. It keeps bringing me back to the fact that our natural state is always there for the seeing—always.

Seen Clearly

Question: Hi, Rodney. The light here in (a city in the U.K.) is beautiful. It belongs neither to summer nor autumn, and has the colours of both. Wonderful! Gorgeous sunsets, too, with shades of pink, which I am not sure I have seen before.

Rodney: Thanks for email and the fine descriptions!

Q: I have settled back into my teaching schedule after the summer break, and I haven't been able to get to my computer as often as I would like. In fact, I feel exhausted already!

Rodney: Pace yourself, drink plenty of water, and get whatever sleep your body requires.

Q: In a couple of weeks, I would like to arrange a phone consultation with you. It will be lovely to talk again!

Rodney: Same here. Just let me know, and we'll work it out.

Q: I just finished enjoying your introduction in John Wheeler's 'Clear In Your Heart'. It's really nice. And very moving!

Rodney: Thanks again. When John asked, I was happy to do it. It's a fine book, and deserves to be savored. I hope you resonate with it. I know that term is used a lot in nondual circles. But it is simply being moved and paused by someone's writing, teaching, or perspective. You may be hard pressed to say precisely what it is that causes you to gravitate to a teacher's words. Nonetheless, the pull is there. And I wouldn't hesitate to go with it.

Q: Well, I certainly find myself doing that. For I have also been continuing to sit with your beautiful pointers in 'A Vastness All Around', letting them open up fully. They all resonate so powerfully. More and more, I am struck by the obviousness and simplicity of the natural state, which is clear until the mind begins to judge, doubt or comment (and even thought is simple until it is invested with meaning).

Rodney: I don't exaggerate when I say that you're so close to this understanding yourself. All of us are "close" all the time, of course. But the easy and clear-sighted manner in which you are naturally and deeply paused by pointers tends to indicate that the person is just a "non-step" away from the actual recognition of his or her unchanging Self.

Q: *"When no thought is present, what is present?" really stopped me yesterday. There was just this luminous knowing of experience—of thought, sensation, perception—and none of it "mine" in the directness of what is presently appearing. Just a Knowing of all this, with no indefinable knower. And this Knowingness has no problems with the (his name) character. He is accepted just as he is, with all his quirks and shyness!*

Rodney: True. And when you come around to a full and sudden seeing of all of this, you will realize that there is no person there to do the accepting! So the term or action doesn't even come up. And neither does it happen. Any time there is any "acceptance" of anything, there is imagined person doing the accepting. I know that there of lots of meditation methods and self-improvement books that involve the use of acceptance; but really, you have to see beyond all of that to if you want to truly find out who and what you are. And what you are is natural state, which is utter peace and immeasurableness. There is no one there to "accept" anything! It is you. So there is nothing for you to do except recognize that, right here and now, you are awareness itself. You absolutely never move from that. Contemplate this fact, with ease and naturalness, and all will be seen clearly.

Utterly Unchanging

Question: I really enjoyed your last pointers. The clarity of your writing shines through so beautifully.

Rodney: Thank you!

Question: And I'm looking forward to our next phone consultation. They have been enormously helpful.

Rodney: Happy to hear it. Such conversations can be appear very ordinary, on one level; and yet, any number of quiet and significant insights can happen if the person you are speaking with has a living understanding of his or her reality. There is also the distinct possibility that seeds will be planted (so to speak), and that some pointer will flourish with clarity at some later time, if the central issues are focused upon.

Question: Right.

Rodney: I mean, you can talk about advaitic/nondual theory all day long—anyone can do that. But how are you helped by it? You are simply left with more questions—even when you are given the answers! And what you want is the opposite of that, where you have no questions whatsoever. And the only thing that leaves you without a single doubt is the discovery of your natural state.

Q: Recently, I have been less and less drawn to the latest nonduality publications. There is really no urge here any more to seek out new books or new authors. Once upon a time, I would have purchased anything and everything, greedily devouring whatever I could!

Rodney: That's great. It shows that you sensing that the answer is more in you, rather than in any particular book. Still, books can be fine pointers, if the writing is direct and clear.

Q: I am happy just to keep coming back—naturally and lovingly—to your own work, John Wheeler's, Randall Friend's, 'Sailor' Bob's, and one or two others maybe. Each relaxed re-reading feels fresh and yields many new insights. There is a subtle and different resonance each time.

Rodney: If you gravitate towards a certain person, teacher, or writer, it's probably worth following that feeling. Again, it all comes back to your resonating with someone, and the manner in which he or she speaks or writes directly about nonduality.

Q: I have been reflecting, too, on this marvelous pointer of yours: "Stay with that which Does Not Move. What is it, right now, that Is Not Changing?"

Rodney: Yes, there is something that is not altering in the least. Yet, it is immeasurable and fully present. What is that something? . . .Well, you are that something! But not you as a separate person, but you as awareness. And if you are awareness at this very moment, your not recognizing it must mean that you are merely overlooking it. It is that simple. And this isn't a theoretical matter in the least. We are talking about what you are existing as at this very second.

Q: Yes. Exploring direct experience right now, it is clear that thought is energy in spontaneous motion, as are feelings, and perceptions. Even the body—which the mind might consider "static"—is really not that at all. If attention is placed on any part of "my" body, what I find is a subtle flux of sensation. Nothing—no object—in experience is still. And yet it is all appearing to something that is utterly unchanging; that does not move at all. Movement is known only against stillness. And ultimately it is not separate from that stillness, either. It is all one.

Rodney: It is all one. There is just this singularity here. And even that isn't quite right, because when we think of a singularity, we tend to think of dimensions, however small, large, or unitary. But awareness is beyond even the notion of oneness. It is more of a "this-ness." And that is all there is, despite any apparent multiplicity.

Q: So if none of that multiplicity (thoughts, feelings, physicalness, etc) is invested with significance, it is so simple! It is the bare presence of aware knowing—that is undeniable, and yet unfindable as any kind of object. It is beyond objects, and yet intimately one with them, inseparable from them. If thought is paused, it is so obvious! And so naturally known.

Rodney: Beautifully put. But just a couple of clarifications: There is no relationship between objects and awareness, however "intimate" that relationship may be. For all things are awareness, even the appearances. And we want to give those appearances due significance, rather than no significance at all. For we want to be able to go to the grocery store and interact with others as smoothly and as safely as possible, while understanding that, fundamentally, there is nothing that is not awareness.

Q: Right now, the sound of my cat crunching his biscuits is no less "me" than the itch on my arm! There is clear and impersonal awareness of both. One is not "closer" to awareness than the other. And although awareness is the intimate substance of sensation/ perception, it also cannot be reduced to them. It is there, with or without objects.

Rodney: Yes, with or without objects. And when there is a pause in thought, no object is present. These pauses are naturally occurring all during day, as well as when you are paused by a nondual pointer. So you do not have to try to stop thought or watch thoughts in order to snatch/gain/merged with presence. Just see that awareness is never not present. Stay with that fact: That awareness is never not present! And that you are it, awareness itself.

Q: As always, thank you, Rodney. I find it so helpful to share insights with you, and to reflect upon your excellent pointers.

A Hushed Spaciousness

Question: Sorry I haven't been in touch for a while. Teaching has been quite tough, and I have managed to catch a stomach virus and the flu in consecutive weeks, which meant that I was off for a few days, and had to catch up when I got back.

Rodney: The flu and a stomach virus!? My God, man! You have got to stay away from those "draughty" English castles and all of that cold morning toast—which, by the way, should be hot and properly slathered with butter before consumption.

Question: Got it! (Laughter). The upside is that it has been a time for reading and walking. The autumnal colours are exquisite here, as well as the light on the turning leaves; it's misty today, too . . . "season of mist and mellow fruitfulness" indeed!

Rodney: Sounds lovely.

Q: I quite understand about your updating your blog once a fortnight now, rather than every week. It must have been exhausting, having to keep going to the hot-spot room in the next building.

Rodney: It was. But you know, I am still going back-and-forth each day, just to keep up with the correspondence and the phone consultations. So it continues to be tiring. But I'm no longer having to go over at such a fever pitch.

Q: I loved the dialogue you posted a couple of weeks ago: "Right now, what is it about yourself that isn't moving or changing in the least?" That is such a potent and beautiful pointer! Every time I go back to it, it is fresh and vibrant.

Rodney: That means you're alive to the depth and significance of self-knowing. Your seeing and sensitivity are such that you are likely to be paused by any excellent pointer, no matter who is it from. And the source, of course, is quite secondary here. The primary issue is your recognizing that you are the pause, that you really do not have to go any further than that to come to this understanding. The answer is right there, in your very own natural and mental halting. There is nothing to process or "work with"—but rather, only to pinpoint.

Q: Actually, all of your pointers appear "new" every time I read them, which is wonderful. That hushed spaciousness is fairly clear now, even with the click-clacking of a train going by, the tapping of my fingers on the keyboard, and the flux of sensations in my body and the chair. This is something that the mind will never get!

Rodney: Precisely, because thoughts have no inherent intelligence. They arise and fall in a kind of supreme intelligence (awareness). But thoughts have no cognitizing power of their own. They are mental appearances, though they can be memory-like, musical-like, and picture-like. Some neuroscientists say that thoughts are merely separate, neuro-chemical reactions. That is fine too. However you label them, they are vital to our living responsibly and communicating effectively. There can also be pointers to our natural state, which is synonymous with that all-pervading "intelligence" that I was speaking about earlier. And we are That. We are not our thoughts. Sometimes I feel like saying this again and again to folks, but you've gotten it clearly. And all that's needed now is a final seeing—

Q: — of that clear and enduring spaciousness.

Rodney: Precisely. When the spaciousness is present and unwavering, that is the recognition of your natural state. And once that is seen, it is seen. Answers naturally begin to fall into place, in terms of any spiritual and conceptual doubts you might have had. It is clear to you now that your inner peace is totally beyond any blissful or visionary experience that you might have had. For you are that living understanding to which Sankara, Gaudapada, Nisargadatta Maharaj, and U.G. Krishnamurti so brilliantly pointed.

Q: Rodney, once again, thank you so much. Take good care . . . We are off in a few days to the Peak District, which is just down in Derbyshire.

Rodney: Oh, lucky folks! Enjoy.

BOOK REVIEW

Review of 'Fully Present: Daily Reflections on Nonduality'

by Gurleen Grewal, Ph.D.

This book belongs in what may be called the sahaj (or nonarduous) lineage of the direct path of inquiry and is good reading for anyone interested in the awakened life.

Fully Present: Daily Reflections on Nonduality is a candid and moving narrative of the quotidian "isness" of 365 days, rendered remarkable in their freshness. Recording both the writing life and the phenomenal world (states of mind and body, thought and feeling, the report of the senses) in unpretentious, expressive prose, the book celebrates the simple pleasures of the discerning palette, as well as a delight in the world of books and music—all of it held in a spacious backdrop of stillness.

Although the personality—with its likes, dislikes, and memory—is registered, this is not the entrenched story of a "me"; but rather, there is simply the noticing of what arises. The journal debunks myths of the spiritual life cherished by seekers, who prolong the search, complicate what is simple, and postpone what is here and now.

Gurleen Grewal, Ph.D., Associate Professor in English, and Director of the Center for India Studies, University of South Florida, Tampa.

Excerpt from Fully Present: Daily Reflections on Nonduality:

Friday, January 15

A word about the diary's title. It comes from Chapter 45 in *Lao Tzu's Tao Te Ching*, which reads, in part:

> *True perfection seems imperfect,*
> *Yet it is perfect itself.*
> *True fullness seems empty,*
> *Yet it is fully present.*

These words beautifully point to the fact that it is not "me" who has become unconditionally present. But rather, there is simply the presence of awareness itself. Indeed, there is the seeing and understanding that awareness has always been unreservedly there. The body and mind are merely appearances in that awareness, and therefore quite secondary (which is not to discount their marvels and uniquenesses). And ultimately, of course, the body/mind too are nothing but presence itself.

Haiku

The Only True Life

"Pretty! Pretty!"
from a deeper, cooler
place in the woods

Kayak excursion—
hovering between the sky
and the sky

Forgetting my debit card's
pin number, I sit outside—
breakfast aromas

Autumn stillness—
a leaf tumbles
to its reflection

Frigid afternoon—
a gust of wind
whitens the water

There are no
jars and pots to fill.
The clay alone is real.

My monthly margarita—
a clarity now
within the inebriation

   Kissing
her pale toes
   in the morning glories

INTERVIEWS

Five Question Interview

This five-question interview was compiled from questions that I have received about *Fully Present: Daily Reflections on Nonduality* since its publication last year.

1) **Why did you write the book?**

I didn't think a nondual diary by a self-realized writer had been done before. But I wasn't trying to "pave the way" or be some sort of "first." I just noticed that such a book, to my knowledge, had not been written, and I was willing to give it a go. Secondly, I wanted to see what came of it myself. For I had no clue what I would be saying. I quickly saw, though, that I wouldn't be able to write daily entries, because of my job and the blog. And finally, I wanted readers to see me how this life of mine had changed, as well as how it had not changed. For example, feelings and emotions continue to arise, but very little is identified with.

2) **What is your favorite entry?**

It wasn't written by me. It's the quote from the movie, *2010: The Year We Made Contact*, at the beginning of the book. And no, I'm not going to repeat it here, because it is much too personal—which is ironic, given that I didn't write it. And yet, it readily and beautifully captures my perspective (or rather, the lack of one) and how life radiates for me these days.

3) **Okay, but you have to have some favorite selections.**

I really don't. Each entry is, at once, deeply intimate and completely impersonal. Each arises from Beingness itself. With that said, I was quite moved by Colleen Loehr's Preface, of course. That she agreed to write it—despite her busy job (a psychiatrist) and hectic family life—was an immensely generous gesture on her part. I am also remembering those 100F-plus degrees of summer, the reflections on Stephen Mitchell's translation of the *Tao Te Ching*, my girlfriend's leaving just after

Thanksgiving, and the subsequent solitary days and nights of the holidays. Why they are presenting themselves as I type these words I have no idea.

4) Do you regret writing anything in Fully Present?

God, yes. And no, I'm not going to list them here. They are done. But for whatever reason, a handful of entries now appear much too private. And one or two, fluffy. I knew that that was likely to happen, but I proceeded with the writing. But most of the entries succeed (in some form or fashion) in what I was attempting to do: Reflect upon the personal in a way that points wholly beyond it. For though the book appears to be about a defined "me," it would be more accurate to say that it is about a lived life, e.g., about the multitude of things that were coming up and disappearing into the beauty, wholeness, and serenity of Presence. That sounds a tad ethereal and intangible, but I don't mean it be. Also, my life is very ordinary, very simple. Anyone looking on would be thoroughly bored by it. And yet, awareness is extraordinary indeed. And that apparent interplay (for the lack of a better word) between the ordinary and extraordinary is one of the hallmarks of this "final understanding."

5) Will there be a Fully Present 2?

I can assure you that there will not be a FP2! This book was nothing but work! "Why or why or why," kept popping into my brain, as I repeatedly tried to capture each day's events. Fortunately, the diary has been of considerable help to some people. And I'm thrilled about that, of course. For if it assists in ending a life of doubt, confusion, and suffering for just a single person, then the book will have served its purpose well.

Assorted Questions & Answers from Blog Readers

Question: Why are you doing your blog every two weeks now? I'm really going to miss your weekly nondual gems!

Rodney: I can't afford wi-fi, and I was exhausting myself by having to go to my apartment's wi-fi hot-spot room in the next building—especially when it was raining or freezing. I would love to have wi-fi, but it does not seem to be in the cards at the moment.

Q: What can I do to speed up my self-realization?

Rodney: Well, there is nothing hindering you from being what you are right now. And what you are right now is awareness itself. Just remain with that glorious fact for a moment. Allow it to pause you fully. You are already awareness at this very moment . . . When that fact is seen or realized, your identity will be clear. There is no practice or process that will catapult you to presence because (once again) presence is your natural state. So nothing can "speed up" the process because you are already That. It is just a matter of seeing or understanding this for yourself, which—of course—not only can happen at any moment, but which takes less than a moment to realize.

Q: How do I send a donation? I really love your work and writing.

Rodney: Thank you. You may send a check or cash—just email me for the address. You may also send a donation via Paypal, where my email address is: srodney00@gmail.com

Q: Once I become enlightened, will I want to quit my job and leave my family?

Rodney: That is highly unlikely. For nothing unusual happens, except the discovery to this unchanging background of deep peace and spaciousness, and the understanding that you are that background. Everything else remains pretty much the same—your allergies, your insomnia, your dessert preferences, and your personality (though you probably will appear generally calmer).

Q: Please give me something to reflect on during the day. I'm not asking for a mantra, just something to slow my thinking and get me going in the right direction.

Rodney: You are already what you are seeking.

Q: Does your sexual drive diminish with enlightenment?

Rodney: Yep, that's the first thing that goes . . .Just kidding! In fact, you will probably find yourself enjoying it more.

Q: How does your natural state feel? And is it there all the time?

Rodney: It's a hushed background of deep peace and spaciousness. And yes, it's there all the time, whether you're noticing it or not. Thoughts and feelings arise and fall, but Presence is ever-present. Other teachers and writers may describe it differently. But for me, the above words come closest to what I'm experiencing.

Q: I like the prominence that you give to OM, which I love to chant. I haven't seen any other nondual teacher mention the word.

Rodney: Well, I don't give it any particular significance. For it has its own prominence: It is the first word in the first Upanishad; it is the substratum of all sounds; and it is perhaps the closest phonetic approximation of Presence that we have. And that some sage or sages recognized these facts even centuries before the Upanishads were written is mind-boggling to me. But that sage discovered it within his or herself first, and then attempted to articulate it. Thus we have OM. I was not there, of course.

But I'll wager that that was how it came about. The important thing here is that you can discover "OM" within your own beingness, just as that teacher, authority, or person did all those centuries ago. Just quiet yourself for a moment and note that the sound is actually present within you right at this moment. But it is not really a sound you are seeking; but rather, the essence of the sound—a sort of hushed, non-moving vibration. I know it appears as if I am talking in riddles. But it is very difficult to describe, especially when you are attempting to be as direct and as accurate as possible.

Q: Should I stop meditating?

Rodney: Only you can answer that question. Continue if you want to continue or if you enjoy meditation. Stop if you feel inclined to do so or if you see that it isn't working for you, in terms of "awakening" you to who and what you are. And don't necessarily stop because I say that recognizing your natural state will not happen that way. For the next 20 or 30-years, test it out for yourself!

Q: I have some strong religious conditioning. Will that hinder me from studying nonduality?

Rodney: You are not your conditioning. You are that which is aware that the conditioning is appearing. Further, the conditioning isn't there in any defined or permanent way. It appears and disappears, appears and disappears. So it can't possibly be you—for you are not something that comes and goes. Right now, what is it about yourself that isn't moving or changing in the least? Remain with that question for a few moments, and it just may well set you free (in the sense that you discover that freedom is your very nature and that that is nothing to attain) . . .As to the second part of your question, nonduality can certainly be historically and philosophically studied. But I sense your question is more from a self-knowing point of view. If that is so, then just be mindful that credible books, blogs, writings, and teachers are always pointing beyond themselves to the readers' or listeners' own innate Freedom.

POINTERS

What is it that does not know your name?

*****

The body, mind, emotions, personality, and consciousness—none of these things is you. So what is it remains? What is it that is in full view but is being overlooked?

*****

Presence is not a void. Indeed, it is the only real thing that there is.

*****

You have to see yourself by yourself. No teacher can "transmit" this understanding to you; neither can the teacher give you some method or process with which this understanding will occur.

*****

When I say "understanding," I mean a direct and simple knowing of your own nature.

*****

See or feel what the pointer is pointing to. The words are nudging you (directionally, not sequentially) towards a peace and silence that has been woefully overlooked. You are that silence! You are that peace! And even those descriptions are concepts on top of this indescribable This-ness.

*****

There is nothing to be done and no one to do it. You can't GI-Joe your way to this understanding.

*****

Stop trying to be free and simply see that you are Freedom itself. How can awareness, which you already are, be in any way acquired? More foolish still is to think that presence can somehow be "entered" or "maintained"!

*****

You are what is being sought.

*****

Who is dissolving what? There are no real characters in this play. All there is is awareness. See the beauty, silence, and unchanging vastness of it. Nothing has to be rehearsed, fine-tuned, or performed. You are what you are at this very moment. You always have been and you always will be.

*****

Awareness is not an experience. It is the background on which all appearances appear. Awareness, when recognized, is perpetual serenity and boundlessness.

*****

Worshipping teachers and checking out the latest techniques are such a waste of time. They quickly come to a stop when your understanding is clear.

*****

The "ego" cannot be dissolved. So forget about that approach all together. For you would be attempting to stop something that naturally occurs and then disappears. It is a practicality that helps you to function in life. Simply bring your attention to the spaciousness in which that "I-sense" comes and goes, and this understanding will be yours.

*****

You are awareness itself. You can't possibly be anything but that.

*****

The body, mind, personality, and consciousness are all arisings in presence. You are not any of those arisings. You are that which knows that those appearances are momentarily there. Bring your attention to the spaciousness surrounding the thought or emotion.

*****

You are the sumptuous and un-altering background to your apparent and ever-changing life. Your very own peaceable kingdom resides squarely within you. And it is a stillness without end. For the space inside of a jar is the same space outside of the jar. The jar is largely inconsequential. The space is not.

*****

Even an ongoing "acceptance of all things" is the "me" in muffled operation. There are no positions to be taken by any apparent "I" when it comes to self-knowing.

*****

Earnestness, graciousness, and purposefulness are qualities that I see, time and again, in seekers who have any measure of success in nonduality. I don't exactly know why that is, but it is a commendable thing nonetheless.

*****

There is no individual. So there is no free will. Thoughts, decisions, and inclinations spontaneously appear in presence.

*****

Right now, what you are is prior to any doubts, questions, and imaginings that you might have about nonduality.

*****

Don't turn self-knowing into a process. If you do, it will certainly be a never-ending one. Why? Because then your focus and attention would be on the methodology, rather than on what is fully and radiantly present. No process can "take" you to awareness. You are that already! So the use of any method to "reach" your natural state is simply idiotic.

*****

Just look and see if you are anything other than this knowing spaciousness.

*****

There is no separate self. You are presence proper. If you reflect upon this, quietly allowing the accuracy of that statement to come to you throughout the day (naturally and spontaneously), you just may come to see the actual and living Truth to which the statement is pointing.

*****

Right at this moment, what is present, aware, and not moving? There is only one thing that has all three of those qualities.

*****

Just because some people assert that they have no more questions, doesn't mean that they have come to a true understanding of who and what they are. This applies to seeker and teacher alike. There has to be a complete seeing of how life is apparently appearing and dividing itself into subjects and objects, forms and no-forms. Otherwise, nothing has been realized.

*****

Consciousness is appearance. It has no inherent intelligence; therefore, it cannot be aware of anything. Something is shining and witnessing through consciousness, and thus giving the impression that it is aware.

*****

Let me be clear: You do not come to this recognition through some sort of experience—no matter how euphoric or blissful that experience may be.

*****

We talk a lot about understanding in nonduality. But actually, self-knowing is totally beyond any conceptual, psychological, or spiritual apprehension. And it is certainly beyond any names or labeling we might attach to it. Understanding, by most credible teachers, simply means a recognition of the presence of awareness within you. And by knowing that it is fully evident, you immediately perceive that there is nowhere where it is not. And that there is nothing that is not. It always is, and it always will be.

*****

Simply see what it is that has never been absent.

*****

Who is standing apart from presence? You certainly are not. All that is happening is that there is a thought saying that you and awareness are somehow separate.

*****

Don't focus on doubts and questions. They are simply passing manifestations in what you already are!

*****

Awareness cannot be experienced. It isn't an object or something new that comes into being. It unequivocally exists, right here and now. Allow these words to resonate within you throughout the day, if you are so inclined. Such contemplations have to be absolutely natural and unforced to be effective.

*****

You can't get any closer to what you are right at this moment. Even when your understanding occurs, there will be no attainment of anything. You will merely (joyously) perceive that presence has always been abundantly present. You will see how beautifully the name directly points to itself!

*****

Your natural state is your natural state. It never moves from being categorically there.

*****

I really don't think of myself as a teacher. That aspect of my life happens naturally. Someone asks a question or writes an email, and I reply. The response is totally natural and spontaneous—and yes, I do tend to go on a bit. But can you ask a flower not to emit its fragrance? No, it just happens. There is no artifice or attempts to impress by the flower. It just spontaneously radiates its beauty and aroma. I could easily sit silently, of course, and say nothing at all about this sublime peace and spaciousness. But you see, to an astute observer, that would be teaching too!

*****

All pointers are conceptual. Yet, the best ones aim away from themselves, to awareness itself. You can't remain with ideas and concepts, and expect to come to this understanding. The same applies with repeating mantras and engaging in practices; for even with those activities you continuing to exists on a dualistic and conceptual level.

*****

You don't have to do a single thing, except perceive what is perfectly present.

*****

You are searching for air when air is all around you. Just breathe in, i.e., perceive that formless presence of peace and spaciousness directly within and before you. You never move from being this hushed whatness and plenitude. So try taking note of how things are constantly changing throughout your daily life, and you just may discern that which is not changing in the least.

*****

What is it, right now, that you do not have to attain?

*****

There is no one there to "accept" or "receive" awareness. Those are false actions regarding a false self. Awareness is what you are and not something that you can "merge" with.

*****

True peace is beyond any steps you think you have to make toward it.

*****

Why strive for "one-pointedness"? You won't get it that way. Just see that one-pointedness is your natural and present state.

*****

Something never moves from being precisely what it is. What is that something?

*****

Becoming "enlightened" is like seeing water in the desert. The water is a mirage. You will never reach it. For the moment you give credence to the notion that awakening is progressive or just ahead of you someplace, you are bound for disappointment.

*****

To say that one liberates oneself is still too much. It is simply a seeing or understanding that "liberation" is your very nature. For awareness is totally without limits or qualities, and you never move from being precisely That.

*****

You can come to this understanding anytime, anywhere.

*****

Meditators, gurus, and false teachers think that you can have a "relationship" with awareness. They believe that you can explore it, expand it, and deepen it. But nothing could be further from the truth.

*****

This understanding has nothing to do with anything that is visionary, ecstatic, mystical, or heavenly. Neither are such occurrences prerequisites for self-knowledge.

*****

You do not have to "expand" your consciousness for self-knowing. That is the mindless "I" going full tilt. And further, that "I" is nothing but consciousness itself! So you have to perceive or understand what is already prior to and beyond it. That is the direct and trouble-free way to your own realization.

*****

True love feels boundless. You can't help but smile and gaze at the person, as well as want to touch and be near him or her. Your entire being is suffused with feelings of warmth, laughter, joy, and gratitude. There is just a natural pouring forth of those feelings, with little regard to one's self-image or perceived individuality. And yet, love too is an arising in presence.

*****

You are seeking something that is never absent.

*****

What you are looking for is the direct experience of your natural state, not some conceptual notion of how that state should be.

*****

Doubts, questions, and reservations are just thoughts! They have no power beyond themselves. Thoughts occur in awareness. So give your attention to the pauses after the thoughts, and see what is being ignored.

*****

Are you aware of being conscious? Yes! And that means that you cannot possibly be consciousness itself. If you are aware of a thing, you cannot possibly be that thing. You are the witness of it.

*****

As you near this understanding, you will probably find yourself having fewer and fewer questions. This is because the idea of any defined "someone" seeking such-and-such will be far less potent. There will just be this gut feeling that you are immensely more than you have imagined yourself to be.

*****

When there is the awareness of a thought, there is no you in addition to that awareness.

*****

All a teacher can do is point, clarify, and encourage. But those are three immensely valuable offerings, especially since they are coming from someone who is actually self-realized. That the person is even taking the time to do this is an extremely compassionate (yet natural) undertaking on the teacher's part. For he or she could just as easily say nothing at all.

*****

You are awareness itself. Once recognized, how could it ever be lost?

*****

Take a careful look at your day-to-day life. What is it that never changes? There is a subtle presence of utter serenity and spaciousness that is yours for the seeing. It has never not been present. It has simply been bypassed. Come to it once, and it is yours. You don't have to re-acquaint yourself with it again and again, in order to deepen or intensify it, though many teachers will have you believe that.

*****

There has to be an earnest seeking for self-knowledge; otherwise, the seeker is likely to be waylaid by occasional and uncommon "spiritual" experiences—or the lack of them. But with earnestness, your own impetus and gravitas sustain you. There is then this unquenchable pull or drive to this final understanding. There is rarely any feeling of being completely disheartened. Rather, there are some days when you aren't drawn to do any reading, listening, and contemplating about nonduality at all. And on other days, the thrust and incentive are there once again.

*****

Just Knowingness and nothing else.

*****

A true teacher points to what is fully present at this very moment.

*****

You are limitless, featureless, cognitizing awareness. You are prior to any concept, belief, and teaching. See the utter foolishness of trying to "reach" presence by pilgrimages and practices.

*****

You are beyond the mind at this very moment! So any attempt to do that would be counter productive and nonsensical. Understand that there has always been a stillness and clarity that were immediately present. Just an easy and subtle recognition is all that is needed.

*****

Can you say that you are not present, as you read these words? No, you are undeniably present. Now look even more attentively, and you will see that what is actually the case is that there is ONLY an ever-abiding existence of awareness, and that you are that awareness.

*****

"I am my body" and "I am my mind" are merely ideas you have about yourself, or things that you have been told. But if you carefully investigate those assumptions (with reason and personal discovery), you may find that they are not true at all.

*****

Your natural and majestic state isn't the production of thought. You can't think or imagine your way to it. But when there is a natural pause in your thinking or imagining, presence is there for the seeing. Awareness is never not there, of course. It only appears to be absent because your attention is elsewhere.

*****

You are what you are at this very moment. And what is that? You are awareness proper. The body isn't aware of itself! But rather, there is an awareness of the body. The simplicity of all of this is nothing less than astonishing.

*****

Some people and teachers speak of awakening as a kind of "inner revolution." But that's a bit strong. For nothing is changed, destroyed, or improved upon with this understanding. You are merely seeing something that has always been in existence. Thus, you can't "practice" your way toward it. For you are Freedom itself. Full stop. Come back to this point again and again, if you feel an inclination to do so. Again, you are awareness itself. And you absolutely never move from that.

*****

My concern is with what you are, and not with any theories or concepts related to what you might think that you are.

*****

The greatest thing that you could ever say about yourself is "I am." Any time you add anything to that—"I am a spiritual person," "I am lazy," I am a Southerner," etc—you are severely limiting yourself. Yes, you certainly want to be able to speak and to communicate with others. But just know that self-limiting thoughts are patently false.

*****

Even questions are a kind of "move away" from your natural state. This isn't to dissuade you from asking them—but rather, to simply see the truth of issue.

*****

A thought can't be aware of itself. And neither can it be aware of other thoughts. So thoughts definitely have their limitations! Further, when no thought is present, something continues to be present. So what is it that never alters from being unequivocally THERE? It is the serene, unbounded presence of your natural state.

*****

After this understanding occurs, the "I" and "me" continue to come up. But they are no longer defined and actual points of reference. They are usages to facilitate communication and comprehension. They come and go, come and go. So they are no more your actual Self than your DVD player.

*****

Don't look for something that you do not already have.

*****

God, Brahman, Enlightenment, Spirituality, the Tao, Buddha-mind, Supreme Freedom, etc, are merely words that point to your core existence. After this understanding is clear, you will probably find yourself using the above terms less and less, if at all. For you'll see that however lovely and venerable the expressions may be, they fail to approximate the infinitude of your inherent nature.

*****

What you are after is the direct experience of your natural state. Anything less than that is of little consequence, spiritually speaking. Self-inquiry ends with the Self. Don't get caught up with needless conjecturing and philosophizing. Such talk is endless and won't bring you one iota closer to presence itself.

*****

Turn your attention not to what is happening, but to what is not moving in the least!

*****

Any pause between thoughts and feelings is an immediate opportunity to perceive your innate tranquility. Don't try to grasp or lengthen the pause. Simply see that there is a very real presence of awareness before and within you. It is limitless and unvarying, and you are That.

*****

When you come to this understanding yourself, you will discover how superfluous self-appointed gurus and spiritual practices are. Even my plunked down in this chair and talking with you is a bit much. But if we stick to the key issues and keep the pointing clear and direct, then some genuine benefit is possible in such discussions. Yes, I could sit here in complete silence, and that, too, would be a legitimate way of expressing this teaching. But who would get it? Who would understand what the silence is directing them to? That is why silent retreats don't work—because the seekers are focused on being silent, rather than on recognizing that to which the silence is pointing. For even silence is an action and an idea. It is in no way related to who and what you truly are at this very moment.

*****

You are awareness itself. It doesn't get any simpler than that.

*****

Because you think that there is something that needs to be done, you are not looking at what is perfectly present. But if you were to bring your attention back to the fact of your naturally being aware of things that are appearing at this moment, you just may see that you are awareness proper.

*****

The mind and body aren't the issue. You are simply bypassing presence, which is there 24/7.

*****

The ego is just a thought or feeling. Don't give it any kind of special significance. It is merely an appearance in presence. It comes, and it goes. You don't. You are what never changes. Stay with the truth and beauty of this fact: You are That which never changes.

*****

Your natural state is serene unboundedness. You never deviate from being precisely that.

*****

See, right now, that you are something other than what you assume yourself to be. You are not your body, mind, or personality. You are the awareness that recognizes that any one of those things are currently present. Reflect upon that. Or see—right now—that there is, indeed, a presence of awareness, in addition to everything that is appearing and disappearing.

*****

U.G. Krishnamurti said it beautifully: "The peace you are seeking is already inside you."

*****

You are imposing a fictitious self upon your body and mind. And when you are told that that is not the way to end suffering, you promptly attempt to control or destroy this re-occurring sense of individuality by meditation, mindfulness, and mantras. In fact, the more the ego appears to be a problem, the harder you meditate. But the ego is not the least bothered by all of that because it is a naturally occurring appearance in the body/mind. (Also, it's not a living thing.) It is the meditation, mindfulness, and mantras that are the odd entities out! That is why people end up meditating for entire lifetimes—because absolutely nothing is getting accomplished!

*****

What is inherently present?

*****

Can a wave remain a wave? It cannot. At some point, it becomes indistinguishable from the ocean from which it arises.

*****

Simply put, there is no you to "access" presence. Neither is there any one to dive deeply into some conceptual "inner body." Presence is bottomless, and it has neither a body nor a beginning. And It is all there is.

*****

The mind is nothing but its contents. You are the cognitizing spaciousness that knows that the contents are appearing.

*****

See for yourself what is unequivocally present. This isn't something that you have to hope to recognize at some later date. And just "who" is hoping to do this? The "who" would only be a thought or a notion. Can a thought know or comprehend awareness? It can't even begin to do that!

*****

One of the problems with meditation is that you focus on either stopping what arises or watching what arises. No wonder people fall asleep—because those are two of the most boring and most non-productive things you can do.

*****

Your ordinary/extraordinary awareness is the answer. Full stop.

*****

Nonduality is about understanding what you are, and not about what practices or methods you should use to reach that understanding. And besides, you can't reach what you already are. Remain with the "whatness," and you will recognized that which has always been in perfect and unchanging abundance.

*****

Right at this moment, what is it that will never be touched by anything that you may experience during the day or evening?

*****

Your hair is growing, your heart is beating, your blood is coursing, and your eyes are seeing. But when does this assumed "you" enter the picture? All of those things are being perfectly done without the assistance of a single defined person. Thoughts are forming and actions are being taken. Do "you" know what your next thought will be? Do "you" know what precisely your next physical action will be? Of course not! Show me your permanent, individual self. It cannot be done. You can only point to actions and appearances—that's all. And your witnessing Self is beyond all of this.

*****

Seekers want to have a "spiritual practice" because it makes them feel special and mystical. But they are in no way touching their true sacredness when they engage in such practices, because actions are all on the level of the mind and "doing." And awareness cannot be journeyed-to. It can only be recognized and understood.

*****

The recognition of the presence of awareness not only clarifies any questions or reservations that you may harbor about it, it transcends those questions. For even before you can frame your query, awareness is fully present. Further, you are that awareness. It is a peace and a sheerness that is always immediately before and within you. Truly, there is never a time when it is missing.

*****

Seeing reveals your nonconceptual reality. There is no seer doing the seeing. There is only the seeing. Now how beautiful is that?

*****

Right now, you are present and you are aware. Though that sounds like two things, it is not. It is simply two aspects of presence-awareness, your nondual truth. Here and now, you are infinitely greater than your body or your mind—or even the stars! You have only to see it for yourself.

*****

Who is looking at what? The "who" is transitory, imaginary even. But awareness (the "what") is not.

*****

Something is transcending your body, your notions, and your sense of individuality right at this moment. Again, the transcending is fully occurring. You are already over and beyond all of the above. Just see this for yourself, instead of attempting to "go beyond" your body and mind through some sort of tactic or process.

*****

Presence is fully present. Take your cue from the word itself and recognize what is thoroughly and unvaryingly existing at this very moment.

*****

This understanding can't be "developed" or "surrendered to." Don't get caught up in these stereotypical aspects of spirituality. Indeed, nonduality is beyond all spirituality because it is speaking about and pointing to not only to your natural state, but to existence itself.

*****

All pointers are pointing to what you are right now.

*****

Yes, awareness is subtle. But once it is recognized, you will wonder how you ever could have missed it. Look right now at this knowingness quality within yourself. That is awareness!

*****

There is nothing to extricate and nothing towards which to move. You are what you are at this very second, and you never shift from that. You only appear to be your body, emotions, and personality because you are temporarily identifying with them throughout the day and evening. But in fact, you are the existence that is knowing that all of those things are temporarily appearing.

*****

Eventually, you have to move beyond the pointers to what you are existing as at this very moment. It is a soft and sudden knowing, and it occurs with neither duress nor methodology.

*****

You are not your body, your experiences, or even your consciousness. So what is left? What is remaining? You are the pause that you are feeling at this present moment. Remain with the pause just long enough to recognize that its stillness and vastness never dissolve. That's all that is needed!

*****

A "full stop" is a natural pause that lends itself to a complete seeing of what has always been in perfect abundance. Even the word abundance isn't quite right because there is nowhere where awareness is not. "All is Brahman," as the Upanishads so beautifully declare. Indeed, if nondual scriptures had to be condensed to one sentence, that would be it. Just substitute (or not) Brahman for Awareness, and the same meaning would hold.

*****

Suffering is created from self-identification. And self-identification primarily occurs with the body, thoughts/emotions, states of consciousness (I am awake, I am sleepy, I am focused, etc), and—ironically—states of happiness. Regarding the latter, we surmise or are taught that happiness is the greatest thing that we can experience in our day-or-day life. Typically, happiness arises when we get something that we want or meet a beautiful person or have some "spiritual" experience. Then, of course, we not only want to have this moment again, we want to have it permanently! Then we go through decades (or even a life-time) of attempting to reach that constant state of happiness. And it is never attained, of course, because happiness is an experience. It comes, and it goes. It is not your natural state, which is unvarying peace and spaciousness. It is important to be clear on the mechanics of suffering; otherwise, it can continue (though less noticeably) even after the recognition of your natural state.

*****

Your very nature is awareness. See the bare fact of what you are.

****

You are not your body. You are That which is aware of your body. What is it, right now, that knows that your body and thoughts are present? Remain with the pause that arises from that question. See that within the pause there is a hushed, knowing, un-altering presence of peace and spaciousness.

*****

"Being Here Now" is merely seeing that that is already the case. There is no movement or "shifting" into that position, as many teachers will have you believe. That expression is just another word for Presence.

*****

It is the immediacy and obviousness of awareness that throws many seekers. But there is no difficulty involved in this understanding. Yes, presence is subtle, but not overwhelmingly so. You don't need to concentrate for X-number of minutes or hours on some abstract, nondual term or concept. Just an easy recognition of an inherent tranquility and expansiveness is all that is needed.

*****

There is practically no psychological suffering here. Physical ailments sure: Lower back pain, chronic insomnia, teeth/gum issues, and various other middling matters. But the psychological makeup—thoughts, emotions, personality, etc—are seen for what they are: Temporary appearances in a true and unconditioned Self.

*****

Awareness is not an experience because it is what you are. And it manifests in the body as equanimity and freedom. But they aren't true experiences because there is no subject-object relationship, and they are always the same.

*****

Self-knowledge is not something that you must "enter" or "re-enter." For when do you ever stop being awareness itself?

*****

Start with what you are: Knowingness. Don't let the word throw you or attempt to overly conceptualize the issue. For if you look closely, you will see that what you are simply knowingness. You are not this body, mind, or consciousness. You are that which Knows that your physicality, thoughts, or states of alertness are appearing. Just stay with the fact of this pointer until it is clear, if you have a natural interest in doing so. See that there is indeed an unchanging presence of clarified Knowingness within you and as you at this very moment.

*****

Your natural state is your natural state. It is there whether you sit comfortably in an easy chair or sit uncomfortably in some contorted position on the floor, while taking deep breaths and holding your palms and fingers in the OM position. You do not move into that state by moving into those positions!

*****

Awareness is what you are. You never move away from that. You are the witness to all the appearances of life. Your thoughts, feelings, sensations, physicalness, and consciousness are all a part of that movement. And anything that changes is an appearance; therefore, it cannot even begin to be who and what you are. So what is it, right now, that is remaining completely as it is? There is something, at this very moment, that isn't altering in the least. What is it? What is that something? Spend some time with this question. Just sit with it, if you are drawn to do so. And you just may see the answer for yourself—an answer that has always, always been radiantly present.

*****

What it is that is not moving in the least?

*****

If the mind could lead us to this understanding, then self-knowledge would simply be a matter of taking a few philosophy courses, engaging in regular debates, learning Sanskrit, and/or subscribing to some mystical series of steps or practices. In short, if the mind could show you your actual Self, you certainly would have seen it by now.

*****

You have to see the absurdity of your seeking.

*****

Who needs to do what? The whatness is already there. Awareness is not only undeniably present, but it is your actual identity. You never move from being precisely That. It is simply a matter of seeing this for yourself. And that recognition takes less than a second!

*****

There are various states of consciousness, but just a single awareness to those states. Consciousness arises, changes, and dissipates within the latter. So don't over-emphasize the role or nature of consciousness. For you are beyond even that!

*****

I am always pointing to who and what you ultimately are. Through reading, listening, consultations, and reflecting, you can become increasingly clear about the immediacy of your own unconditioned nature. (Though this isn't to suggest that there is a progressive path or practice to it.) It is there for the seeing. At no time is it distant, hidden, or unavailable.

*****

Awareness is so immediate that you are merely overlooking it. So what is it that you aren't seeing? The question beautifully and automatically pauses you. And that pause is pointing to the answer. Again, what is it that you are not seeing? What is it that you had not noticed before but that is fully and unequivocally present?

*****

This understanding is not gradual. Yes, certain issues may be clarified over one's lifetime. But there is no maturation on the part of presence. What does appear to occur, however, is a deep recognition that experiences are transitory. Thus, you are likely to find yourself savoring a moment while—at the same time—completely letting it go. Or rather, there is the understanding that it is fleeting. For there is no one there to let it go!

*****

Right at this moment, what is the presence that your mind and thoughts are not creating? What is the presence that is already there?

*****

Though consciousness is an appearance, it is only through consciousness and the body that awareness is able to cognitize itself. Absolute awareness is not aware of itself. From consciousness and the brain come thoughts and the notions of a separate "I" and individual person.

*****

You are what you are: Unequivocal awareness! And your inherent nature Does Not Change. Thus, there is no where to go and nothing to get.

*****

Your own direct experience of what you are is what frees you from the notion that something needs to be done to grasp or garner liberation. Your very nature is 100% liberated! Even individualistic thoughts about yourself can't suppress Self in any form, shape, or manner.

*****

Any action towards awareness is just idiotic.

*****

The only thing that you can truly say about yourself at this moment is, "I am." It stops right there. And even that's an overstatement because all there is is "Amness." But that term might be too theoretical to seekers, too far-flung. So go back to the original pointer, if you resonate with that. Discover the undeniable fact of this "I am."

*****

So long as you feel that you have to "get enlightened," you are anticipating—you are mentally projecting that which has already taken place. You are pure awareness at this very second. So what is there to be done? And who wants to do what? And why? You are operating solely on procedural and conceptual levels when there is a "who" involved in self-knowing.

*****

Nonduality points you to timeless, life-changing insights.

*****

Something is aware right now. And it is aware without an object—that is, without a thought, feeling, or sensation. A thought or emotion may arise, but it is largely inconsequential. Zero in on that perpetual presence of peace and spaciousness. Once seen, you will wonder how you ever missed it.

*****

The thought "I am in bondage" is silly; and the thought, "I am Freedom" is redundant, even though it is pointing to the truth. The thing to see here is that you are not your thoughts at all!

*****

Awareness, your true nature, is all there is.

*****

This understanding is not some higher-level of consciousness or anything like that. Consciousness remains pretty much the same, and awareness is totally beyond it, as I have said any number of times here. So any activity or practice that promises "advanced" levels of alertness and knowingness are still on the level of the mind, not matter how many psychic or expansive experiences you may have.

*****

The Self does not "unfold." It is simply recognized in all of its glory.

*****

Metaphysical exercises are as nonproductive for self-realization as methods and disciplines. But if you are drawn to explore these things, do so. Enjoy your life. And perhaps one day, you will see that so-called liberating practices do not liberate. As the sixth-century Zen master Sosan said in his The Book of No Mind, "When you try to stop activity to achieve passivity your very effort fills you with activity."

*****

Take a moment to see what has always, always present. You are placing all of your emphasis on your mind, and the mind is not the issue. You are focusing on the wrong thing. All spiritual seekers the world over are focusing on the wrong thing. Your mind (if it is neurologically sound and sane) is not the problem. Rising thoughts and emotions are a normal part of your functioning. You simply are not seeing that awareness is present. Thoughts and feeling are present also, but they come and go. Awareness, however, is fully present, and it never alters, evolves, or vanishes.

*****

Yes, we are all one. But what is that oneness? What is that singularity that is in each transitional body and mind? You see, if you merely say that we are all one, it's theoretical. You are just throwing words around. But when you actually attempt to see and understand that magnificent principle that is within each one of us, then the investigation becomes engaging and energetic.

*****

You don't need to try to step out of the "stream of thinking." You are already out! You are continuing to believe the assumption that you are the thinker when you're employing some practice or effort to step out of the stream. Again, you are already out! Thoughts happen within you, not to you!

*****

Go beyond all muddling concepts and spiritual distinctions. Do you really think that your natural state is Buddhist, Advaitic, Christian, or Taoist? Is some smidgen of it any one of these things? No. It is wholly nondual, and thus beyond all categorizations that can be placed upon it.

*****

Thoughts and feelings come and go. But something doesn't. What is that something?

*****

You never move from being absolute awareness. That is the ultimate truth. That is a pointer that pauses you because of its pronounced clarity and simplicity. Reflect upon that truth throughout the day. See that there is nothing to get, because you are awareness already. Don't make the reflection mechanical or even contemplative! Just see the actuality to which the words are pointing.

*****

Do you really think that your doubts, beliefs, and philosophical views affect awareness? Presence doesn't care in the least whether you curse it or praise it. Even your eventual recognition of it will not bring forth any Indic Hosannas or Pentecostal spirituals (though you may find yourself unconsciously moving to anything by the Staple Singers!).

*****

You are the presence that is already beyond all thinking. Now when I say "beyond," I obviously don't mean that it is something that you have not yet gotten. I also don't mean that you have to somehow ascend to it or go in some direction towards it. Yes, you have to see your Self for yourself. But that could not see easier, I promise you. It only appears tricky because you are awareness already. So there is nothing to see as object. All that you can do (or that is needed) is the recognition of your own presence of peace and spaciousness.

*****

What is it that you are not shifting from?

*****

The answer is not in thought. Something knows that the thought is present. Come back to that something. It is a sheer and unvarying reality that is with you right now. There is nothing conceptual or "far off" about it at all. It's just a matter of honing in on what is already emitting the most beautiful of sounds.

*****

Talking with someone who has come to this understanding is an excellent way of clarifying nonduality issues. You may not come to a direct seeing, right then and there. (And then again, you may do precisely that!). Either way, you are bound to have some choice insights and ideas over which to ponder.

*****

What is the presence of awareness that is present right now, as you carefully read these words? . . .Again, what is the presence of awareness that is present right now, as you slowly peruse this sentence?

*****

Yoga, music, and medicine are three things that can be beautifully practiced. Self-knowledge cannot be practiced. The understanding is either there or it is not. But there is much to be said for the spiritual seeker who is unfazed by any apparent bafflement or perplexity on the advaita or nonduality. He or she innately knows or has been told by a credible source that that bafflement is indeed only a notion or impression, and that there is never a time when he or she is not awareness itself.

*****

What you want to be alert for is the presence of what appears to be ordinary stillness. Then take a moment to notice that that stillness actually never moves. It is immeasurable and beginningless. And it is your true Self.

*****

There can be no "progressive dismantling" of the ego. It may seemingly take some time to directly see this for yourself. But the issue of the ego not being a defined entity (but rather a reoccurring sense-of-self) can be recognized at any moment. No specific duration is needed. Because you think time is required to do the dismantling, you are giving undue credence to it and a fictional ego, both of which are not a factor in your understanding.

*****

You are free. Indeed, you are freedom itself. Full stop!

*****

Awareness is neither in some vaulted, architectural wonder nor around some corner. On the other hand, it is in those places also! There is, of course, no place where awareness is not. So the only pilgrimage that needs to be made is an inner one, and that automatically occurs when you naturally and knowingly come to a full conceptual stop.

The Only True Life

*****

Phone Consultation Excerpt:
If I had had some knowledgeable source early on to say to me, "You don't have to do that," that person would have been absolutely priceless. Everyone was saying do this and do that. Do! Do! Do! And nothing worked. Nothing. It didn't even work for them!! So right from the start, there was this tremendous waste of time, energy, and money—money that I did not have. So to have had some kind and knowing soul tell me, "You don't have to do that" would have curtailed an enormous amount of struggling and confusion. Fortunately, today, you have a handful of credible and accessible teachers (on the Web, Skype, and doing actual talks) who are saying, in no uncertain terms, that methods, practices, approaches Do Not Work—that you are what you are before, during, and after any technique in which you may indulge. So how is any meditation session—however long and meticulous— going to bring closer to what you already are? It is not going to happen. It just isn't going to occur. Even the question of "how" do I see this or "how" do I come to this understanding is a movement in thought, a rising wave of duality. Thus, your attention is shifting away from presence at the very start. So come back to some of the fundamentals of this issue. What is Self-realization? It is the simple recognition that you are awareness, itself—that you are the very thing that you are seeking! So take a moment to remain with that pointer and pause, and see where it leads you.

*****

An idea is a concept is a doubt is a thought. You are none of these things.

*****

Your own inner stillness is the answer to what you are seeking. That is it. You feel that stillness any number of times throughout the day, but you give it very little heed or attention (not that it requires undue effort or concentration to discover). The next time you are paused by a passage in a book or a nature scene or by someone's beauty or kindness, stay with the pause just long enough to see that you actually never move from it!

*****

Fraudulent teachers go on and on about bliss and happiness. Real teachers simply point to your natural and overlooked state.

*****

Why do you have to "practice" nonviolence? Why can't you just see that violence is not necessarily the solution? Or that in certain situations, a stronger response may indeed be needed. Let circumstances be your guide. Any time you begin to "practice" something (in spiritual terms), there is an imagined person doing the practicing.

*****

Gurus and non-realized teachers love to go on and on about how "long and arduous" one's "spiritual journey" has to be. But that is how it is for them! And they want you to join them so you can compare difficulties, experiences, and "new beginnings" in some expensive group setting. Stay clear of such people if you have any serious interest in self-knowing. You'll be all the better for it.

*****

Freedom is recognizing that you are Freedom itself. You do not have to become free from a single thing. That perceived individual that you take yourself to be is merely a concept that you have about yourself. But before the concept arises, what is it that is already there? Not who, but what? Just sit with that for a few moments, for it points to your very essence. Again, not who, but what?

*****

As long as you continue to believe in your thoughts, suffering will continue.

*****

To think of yourself as a "divine person" still entails an assumed separation from awareness. Just keep coming back to the point that presence is, and that you are that—or rather, That, as the sages orate. And even "That" is merely a term directing you to your natural state.

*****

There is no one who can attain enlightenment or be liberated because awareness is all there is!

*****

Is there a thinker? Or are there only thoughts, saying that "I am the thinker?" And because we form a memory of that particular thought, we assume that there is a mind that is somehow housing the thinker and multitude of thoughts. But thinking is merely (and marvelously!) happening. There is no thinker—just thoughts, appropriately occurring, one after the other. You are not at the wheel. Indeed, there is no one at the wheel! Everything is fully automated, pretty much like those amazing driverless cars from Google!

*****

There is no "shift" to the immeasurable. It is simply a matter of discovering—instantly and unequivocally—that awareness has always been fully present, and that you are that presence. And when you see this for yourself, it will be as clear and as evident to you as your very own breathing.

*****

How can a prolonged concentration on anything be good?

*****

Be careful about being overly enamored with any words, terms, or descriptions about Beingness. The map is not the territory, and neither is any expression about your natural state. Presence is what you are, and the word is merely directing you to that fact. So allow your attention to follow the direction in which the descriptions and expressions are pointing. And you just may find clarity itself.

*****

It is merely a matter of seeing the simplicity of all of this. Presence is what you are. Therefore, you can neither attain it nor grasp it. You are that as you are reading these words. So fortunately, this isn't something that you can "hope" to acquire at some future date.

*****

I love this illustration by Bob Adamson: "Now, right now, you are hearing and seeing. Does the hearing say, 'I hear'? Does the seeing say, 'I see'?" No. What says those things? The mind!

*****

You not only never move from being what you are, you never move, period! Remain with the pause that that pointer instills. You are that which never alters in the least! So the recognition of this eternal state of yours is simply a matter of discerning what it is, right here and now, that is Not Moving.

*****

If you could magically stop your thoughts for the next hour, you would not be helped one iota. All you would notice is a kind of void, a nothingness. You still would have to recognize the presence of awareness within that apparent void, which you could just as easily do as you are reading these words.

*****

What is it, right now, that you do not have to attain?

*****

You say that you are trying to "reach" or "merge with" the Absolute. But awareness/presence is the Absolute. And it is the only thing there is! The seeker is an idea, a notion, and a falsehood. It has to be seen through or understood in order for self-realization to occur.

*****

What is present before your next thought is present?

*****

You can never "align" with "the Now" (if by "now" you mean awareness, presence, Self, Brahman, the Ultimate, etc). You—the perceived person—will always be behind it, so to speak. Indeed, awareness is completely beyond space, time, and causality. So any teaching that advises or promises "alignment" just isn't going to work.

*****

Awareness is there—but not like your body, emotions, or sensations are there. These are manifestations that come and go. Awareness is more of a background or presence. Focus on these two qualities within yourself that are fully in place right now. Thus, you are not trying to "get" anything; you are merely recognizing something that has never not been directly in front of you.

*****

Ultimately, "Who am I?" is the wrong question. You are not a "who." You are a what.

*****

Again, you cannot "free the mind from thinking." That is just utter nonsense. I don't care how lovely or spiritual it sounds. That is not going to happen—until, that is, you are dead or in some profound coma of some kind. And it's all beside the point anyway; for there is a natural space between each thought, and you are that space.

*****

You are on the lookout for a sheer and beginningless backdrop that is ever-present and is ever-serene.

*****

There is no individual to "stay in the present moment." What is going to happen is that a thought or feeling or sensation is going to arise in that moment, and you are going to assume that it is you. But you—your true self—are that moment. You are the witness, not the manifestation. You are the knowing spaciousness that, heretofore, you have merely overlooked.

*****

Any gradual path or practice leading to awakening is a massive waste of time and energy.

*****

The mind is just arising thoughts. Clarity on this issue will quickly reveal further insights, leading perhaps to self-realization itself. But I am not speaking about any kind of progression here. Any single insight or discernment could easily bring about a full seeing of who and what you are.

*****

In reality, there is no moving nearer or away from awareness. It remains firmly in place, whether you recognize it is there or not.

*****

The "play of life" is actually the play of appearances—things that seem to exist for a certain while and then disappear (whether that duration is a nanosecond or 10 billion years). But anything that has a beginning and an end cannot, under any circumstances, be who or what you are. Remain mindful of that fact as you go about your daily activities or when want to sit in contemplation with this pointer or some nondual issue.

*****

Self-realization is about seeing and understanding, not doing. Awareness is totally beyond all causality. Totally! So how can any action or ritual or practice take you there? If I could give you a glimpse of this truth—from my vantage point—you would roar with laughter at your own actions. But then, a glimpse is all you would need to see and understand that presence is your natural state.

*****

Close your eyes. Forget that you have a body and a mind. Forget even that you are consciously awake at the moment. Let all those things be temporarily absent. Now, what is it that you cannot negate? Allow yourself to see and feel this . . . Once you think that you do, slowly open your eyes. Again, what is it that you still cannot negate?

*****

You say that you meditate, but meditation never stops. You say that you pray, but true prayer never ceases. You say that you chant, but the song of Existence is ever-present. Hear the music for yourself. Take note of any or all of this. Nothing could be simpler.

*****

The knowledge of awareness is the same as awareness. There is no "one" knowing it.

*****

You are That for which you are searching. Allow the sheer beauty and significance of this to halt you in your tracks. Again, you are already that for which you are seeking. You needn't go any further than what you are, right here and now. What is it that you are feeling as you reading these words? Take note of that clear and subtle hushness within you. That is your treasure, your natural and radiant state.

*****

Guided meditations are such comical fluff. Seekers crave them because they can just sit or lie there and "do" something "spiritual." And teachers love them because they fill up the hour and pad the program. Can you imagine Nirsagadatta Maharaj leading a guided meditation? I don't think so! Every word that a true teacher utters is a meditation or a pointer to your true Self. It is merely a matter of noting its significance.

*****

There is no bondage. There is only awareness. Again, there is no bondage. There is only the false thought that "I am bounded" or that "I am a seeker."

*****

Right now, there is something about you that is not moving in the least. What is that something? . . .You are the pause that just answered that question. See the ease and magnificence to that: You are the pause that answered the question! Any transitional word that you may use—whether it be God, Brahman, Allah, the Absolute, the Most High, etc,—is okay. It's just not the actual answer. It is a conditional response to presence itself, which is the living answer and which harbors no labels or conditions whatsoever.

*****

Complete acceptance requires no acceptance whatsoever. You aren't even aware of it happening! A thought, feeling, sensation, or situation appears, and it is either smoothly registered or it causes a conflicting thought or emotion to arise. But again, it is just another appearance. So when you understand all of this from the appearance end (rather than the "acceptor" one), the mechanics of it are easier to grasp.

*****

Stay with the fact that you and awareness are synonymous. It isn't something toward which you can move. You are that very thing, right here and now. Perhaps you are feeling a momentary stillness within you. That's excellent, because it means that you are being attentive to not merely the words, but to how the words are making you feel. Again, you and awareness are the very same thing. So what is it that you are feeling?

*****

The mind is duality. That is why any attempts to come to this understanding through learning Sanskrit, philosophical discourse, or progressive actions (which are product of thoughts) are all for naught.

*****

Excerpt From Phone Consultation:
Who is doing what? You see, that's the question that should naturally arise when you are engaged in any sort of practice or technique to "achieve" self-knowledge. Who is doing what? The question should come up because you are utilizing two unfortunate notions: A perceived individual and an action "towards" what you perceive to be is enlightenment. But those two notions have nothing whatsoever to do with self-realization! You can't get there through either the "me" or the actions/practices of the "me." Nothing! The only way that final understanding is going to occur is when, while doing those actions and techniques, you simply see their futility and stop, just as the Buddha did. Further, if goal-oriented meditation didn't work for Buddha, Nisargadatta Maharaj, U.G. Krishnamurti , Atmananda Krishna Menon, Ramana Maharshi, or Bob Adamson, or John Wheeler (just to cite a handful of examples), why on earth are you even bothering with it yourself!? Not ONE of those teachers "meditated" their way to self-realization! Not a single one! So how is it going to possibly work for you? Even Jesus said that "the Kingdom of God is within you." And he meant that it is within you at this very moment! That is the part that theologians and spiritual seekers don't focus upon: Your inner "Kingdom of God" is within you at this very second. This very second! It is neither in Heaven nor on the other side of some torrid desert. And you require neither time nor techniques for this glorious recognition and understanding.

*****

The seeker is imagined. The sought is already present.

The Only True Life

*****

One of the many beauties of our natural state is that it isn't transcendent at all. It is right here and now, in our everyday life and commotion. That is not to give scant attention to its quiescence and freedom. For those elements are definitely there! It is just that there is an evenness to it that is ever-refreshing.

*****

Everyone is looking, but few are actually seeing. But that lack of recognition is due, in large part, to the obviousness of awareness and not to its obscurity.

*****

"You do not need to meditate." ~ H.W.L. Poonja (aka, Papaji)

*****

Gaze into your own emptiness. And by gaze, I mean to simply take a calm and direct look at it. If you do it just right, you will see a presence of peace and expansiveness that you have simply neglected to notice up to now. Further, that presence, once fully discerned, never disappears—whether you are raking the leaves, having a disagreement with your partner, or enjoying a cup of tea or coffee. So take a calm and direct look at that which is never lost.

*****

This understanding has nothing whatsoever to do with getting the mind and the ego to surrender to some ultimate reality. There is an ultimate reality, of course. And it is ever-present. But the mind and ego are not always present; therefore, they are appearances in presence. So why focus on appearances when they have nothing to do with your natural state?

And who would the assumed person be that would be doing the surrendering?

*****

Your body, mind, and reasoning aspects work splendidly in your practical, everyday life. Ditto love and passion. They are to be nurtured, in a natural and healthy manner. Just know that these are limited forms of living, and they are in no way comparable with functioning from the limitlessness of presence.

*****

Though OM is often chanted by seekers and extolled in the scriptures, it cannot be expressed by any sound.

*****

If you have an opportunity to talk with someone who has come to recognize his or her natural state, by all means do so. Chances are, you will feel a hushness and quietude within yourself as you are conversing. You may not be able pinpoint exactly where that quietude is, but that's not important. The important thing is that you are tuning towards your very own vastness.

*****

How can you "journey" to what you already are? That pointer stops you cold. Or rather, it halts the mind from thinking that it must do something to get enlightenment. Now there are four things that are in error there: The assumed "I", the action of the assumed "I", the notion that you are in bondage, and the belief that enlightenment is something that is attained. So come to the question calmly, and allow it to fully answer itself. How can you journey to what you already are?

*****

There is no such thing as the mind apart from thought.

*****

At this particular moment, what is it that is knowing that your body is present? And again, it is a "what" and not a "who." And that whatness appears as—among other things—unchanging peace and spaciousness. You can't even say that it is teeming with space and equanimity because those are quantifiable terms. And your natural state is wholly without measure. Just a little clear-seeing here is all that is needed.

*****

Only the mind, ego, or sense-of-self causes you to think that a process or practice is needed for self-knowing. But nothing could be further from the Truth, literally speaking. This understanding comes suddenly and quietly (though it may occur in the most frantic of times and places). And no preparation, duties, or code of morals are necessary for it to occur. And why would there be? For you are what you are, as you read these words. And what you are is nothing less than awareness itself.

*****

All suffering (except physical) comes from the notion of a separate "I" or "me."

*****

Even before self-inquiry begins, you are already the Self-awareness proper. Allow the clarity and significance of this fact to pause you into your own understanding.

*****

Really question the assumption that there is a separate self. Where is this separate, individual person? If you point your body, that can't be you because the body is constantly changing. The same applies to your brain, personality, and consciousness. All of those things are appearances and are constantly altering. So again, where is this separate self? What is the first response to that question? The first response is silence—stillness. Then a thought arises, saying, "What else could there be?" or "Man, forget all of this!" The thought really isn't that important. But the stillness is. Go back to that silence, to the first response. It was you! It was actually what you are! The subsequent thoughts were the assumed you. So go back to that pause, and have a clear and direct look at yourself.

*****

Your body, thoughts, and feelings are all arisings. But what is it that is not arising? What is it that is fully present, but is not moving or arising in the least?

*****

Habits, cultivation, devotion, and self-improvement are all activities of the mind. There are in no way related to self-knowledge.

*****

Three things to know: Your body is being lived (you aren't the operator); thoughts and feelings are being formed through the interrelated actions consciousness, the brain, and various other neurological processes (you do not choose or direct your thoughts); and awareness is the witness of these actions and appearances within itself (and you are that awareness).

*****

At bottom, "awakening" and "enlightenment" are notions and concepts themselves. For you are unlimited freedom, even as you read these words! You don't become freer when self-realization occurs. You simply recognize that you are and have always been this immeasurable presence of peace and Beingness.

*****

Right here and now, what is it that is not changing one iota?

*****

Consciousness is the first appearance out of awareness. From consciousness come thoughts and feelings, which cause us to infer duality, e.g., "I am an individual," "I am Alaskan," "I am a spiritual person," "I am not a spiritual person," etc. But you actually never move from being infinite awareness.

*****

Drop all questions and see what it is that is undeniably present. There is no "correct" way for doing this; for that would imply a path or process or procedure. But nonduality is all about what is right here, right now; and thus, no process is needed. Take a calm and careful look at what is enduringly present at this very moment. Once it is seen, you will wonder how you ever missed it!

*****

Descartes said, "I think, therefore I am." But a far more accurate statement would be, "I am, therefore there is thinking." But yes, the former statement is far catchier!

*****

What is it that you are not seeing? . . .Let this be the question that you reflect upon throughout the day or evening, whenever the question naturally arises . . .What is it that you are not seeing? The query pauses you, and you are the pause—the eternal pause that is without beginning or end. And that pause is never not there . . .What is it that you are not seeing?

*****

"There is a stillness / simpler than silence / a peace deeper than calm." ~ Svein Myreng (Plum Poems)

*****

I encourage you to see your Self for yourself. Then all doubts, seeking, and suffering are effectively resolved. For you will realize how self-evident your natural state has always been. Absolutely nothing was ever hidden or at a remove.

*****

Only your mind, ego, or sense-of-self causes you to think that a process or practice is needed for you to be become self-realized. But nothing, quite literally, could be further from the Truth. This understanding comes suddenly and quietly. No duties, preparation, or code of morals are necessary for the seeing. And why would there be? For you are what you are, as you read these words. And what you are is nothing less than awareness itself. And nothing could be more wonderful.

Made in the USA
Middletown, DE
17 July 2019